# FEELING GREAT WITH THE
# MOON

## A Guide to Activating Your Cosmic Energies

REDFeather
MIND | BODY | SPIRIT

## IRENE LAURETTI

**Other Schiffer Books on Related Subjects:**

*Claiming Your Power Through Astrology:*
*A Spiritual Workbook* by Emily Klintworth, ISBN: 978-0-7643-5272-0

*Astrology's Hidden Aspects: Quintiles and Sesquiquintiles* by Dusty Bunker,
ISBN: 978-0-7643-5543-1

Type set in Zurich/Minion

ISBN: 978-0-7643-5618-6
Printed in China
Published by Red Feather Mind, Body, Spirit
An imprint of Schiffer Publishing, Ltd.
4880 Lower Valley Road
Atglen, PA 19310
Phone: (610) 593-1777; Fax: (610) 593-2002
E-mail: Info@schifferbooks.com
Web: www.schifferbooks.com

For our complete selection of fine books on this and related subjects, please visit
our website at www.schifferbooks.com. You may also write for a free catalog.

Schiffer Publishing's titles are available at special discounts for bulk purchases
for sales promotions or premiums. Special editions, including personalized
covers, corporate imprints, and excerpts, can be created in large quantities for
special needs. For more information, contact the publisher.

We are always looking for people to write books on new and related subjects. If
you have an idea for a book, please contact us at proposals@schifferbooks.com.

FOR THE MAN I LOVE.

# CONTENTS

Foreword by David M. Montgomery     7

Is There a Key to Well-Being, Total Health, and Eternal Youth?     9

The Mystery of Soul, Energy, and Vibration Explained through the 9 Depths of Being     10

From the Nothing to the Spiritual Light of Truth and Potential: The Universal Depths 9, 8, 7     11

The Individualization of Unity through the 6 Depths of Individual Being     13

The 12 Soul Gates and the 12 Organ Flows to Create Your Reality!     16

How to Activate the Code of Creation     21

Activating Your Life Flow, Your Personal Source     23

Unfolding Your Star with the Moon and What It Means to Be *In Tune*     28

**Unfolding Your Star for Health, Happiness, and Success!**     47

**6TH DEPTH—SPIRALING CIRCLE**     49

The Moon Opens the Cosmic Gate of **SAGITTARIUS** ♐
*You Open Your Sagittarius Soul Gate through the Vibration of Diaphragm Function Energy*     55

The Moon Opens the Cosmic Gate of **CAPRICORN** ♑
*You Open Your Capricorn Soul Gate through the Vibration of Umbilicus Function Energy*     67

**3RD DEPTH—GREEN POINT-OF-STAR**     77

The Moon Opens the Cosmic Gate of **AQUARIUS** ♒
*You Open Your Aquarius Soul Gate through the Vibration of Gallbladder Function Energy*     85

The Moon Opens the Cosmic Gate of **PISCES** ♓
*You Open Your Pisces Soul Gate through the Vibration of Liver Function Energy*     95

**2ND DEPTH**—WHITE POINT-OF-STAR     105

The Moon Opens the Cosmic Gate of **ARIES** ♈     113
*You Open Your Aries Soul Gate through the Vibration
of Lung Function Energy*

The Moon Opens the Cosmic Gate of **TAURUS** ♉     121
*You Open Your Taurus Soul Gate through the Vibration
of Large Intestine Function Energy*

**1ST DEPTH**—YELLOW POINT-OF-STAR     131

The Moon Opens the Cosmic Gate of **GEMINI** ♊     137
*You Open Your Gemini Soul Gate through the Vibration
of Stomach Function Energy*

The Moon Opens the Cosmic Gate of **CANCER** ♋     145
*You Open Your Cancer Soul Gate through the Vibration
of Spleen Function Energy*

**5TH DEPTH**—RED POINT-OF-STAR     155

The Moon Opens the Cosmic Gate of **LEO** ♌     161
*You Open Your Leo Soul Gate through the Vibration
of Heart Function Energy*

The Moon Opens the Cosmic Gate of **VIRGO** ♍     169
*You Open Your Virgo Soul Gate through the Vibration
of Small Intestine Function Energy*

**4TH DEPTH**—BLUE POINT-OF-STAR     177

The Moon Opens the Cosmic Gate of **LIBRA** ♎     183
*You Open Your Libra Soul Gate through the Vibration
of Bladder Function Energy*

The Moon Opens the Cosmic Gate of **SCORPIO** ♏     191
*You Open Your Scorpio Soul Gate through the Vibration
of Kidney Function Energy*

Congratulations!     199

Be the Cosmic Code of Creation!     201

Symbols and Abbreviations     205

Endnotes     206

# FOREWORD by DAVID M. MONTGOMERY JOHNSTON

Biologist BSc (Hons) and Lifestyle Guru

With this book, dear reader, you are invited to embark on a Soul journey beyond the confines of your physical world and travel to the very origins of your being.

Do not worry; this will come naturally because you, as the seeker, will be guided by the light of truth to comprehend the essential relationship between energy, matter and the Soul, and how these vibrations interrelate and correspond via our vital organs, the elements, and signs of the zodiac.

Containing a totally new interpretation of the Moon and combined with the wisdom of ancient medicine, this book contains a most excellent practical method for you to use to optimize your daily health and fulfilment.

This work is a superb achievement, which is essential and totally in tune with the spirit of today. By the simple fact that you are reading this you have started that process and can know that you have already begun this wonderful journey.

# Is There a **KEY** to **Well-Being,**
# Total **HEALTH,** and Eternal **YOUTH?**

Is there a key to total wellbeing, health, and eternal youth? A key "free of charge," available to everybody to use any time?

A key that is free for the taking—a birthright for you and anybody who wants it? Any time . . . any place . . . and with immediate effects? A key that brings a bright light into your life, miraculously enlightens and transforms your body as well as your whole life, restores total HEALTH, and makes you feel better and younger the longer you use it?

YES, this key exists, dear reader. It has been in front—or more precise *within* you all of the time, etched into your subconscious.

This key is the Moon, or rather your understanding of your SELF through the vibration of the MOON.

> *Your body exists because of and through the vibration of the Moon.*
>
> *Your Soul needs the Moon's vibration to incarnate and construct her reality!*

The Moon is Earth's satellite, companion, and consort. Without it, the world would not exist, you would not be as you are, and you would in fact not even be here at all. In the vast orchestration that has led to life on Earth, the Moon has been a lens and a mediator through which life has manifested. It is through the vibration of the moon that we have incarnated and are nurtured in the world, and by harmonizing with this vibration, we can finally access the key humanity has been searching for since the origins of man.

Sound strange to you?

In order to understand the true importance of the Moon—and most importantly how to "use the Moon"—it is imperative that you get an understanding of **energy** and **vibration**, or rather, of how the visible world—and thus your body and your reality—is created through the merging of cosmic energies that constantly surround you and that in fact YOU yourself ARE.

So, let's have a look at who you really *are*, or rather how you become what you are in this world and what the Moon has to do with how you present your SELF and how you perceive your reality.

In order for you to grasp the principles of the SOUL, energy, and vibration, I will explain "energy" and the laws of creation through the concept of the 9 Depths as used in the ancient Japanese Healing Art Jin Shin.

# The Mystery of **SOUL, ENERGY, and VIBRATION**
## Explained through the 9 Depths of Being

Have you ever wondered what your Soul is, or rather, *who YOU really are?*

What is it that "feeds" you with life, and where have you really come from? What is your "true home"?

The answer is: your **Higher Self**, or, to put it in macrocosmic terms, the level of Unity and Truth.

The level of Unity is the **God-level**, the level above time and space, which encompasses all the other levels, or "Depths," as they are called in Jin Shin. It is that level that has always been and will always BE and out of which reality is born in a constant flow of Life, the **Life Flow**, also known as the "Main Central Flow" in Jin Shin, or the Microcosmic Orbit in Taoism.

The level of **Unity and Eternity**, in other words, is your **Higher Self**. It is the true YOU that you always are but who you may nevertheless not always be aware of, since it is the level above manifestation that cannot be seen with our physical eyes but which leads us to the most important principle in energy healing and creation:

The fact that . . .

# MATTER FOLLOWS ENERGY,

which means that your body, as well as nature and the whole of *reality*—anything you can physically "see" and "touch"—is in truth the ever-changing and evolving **product** of a driving force and energy behind it.

If you manage to understand and harness this *energy,* not only will you be able to understand your SOUL, but more importantly, you will be able to **consciously create your reality** *through* your Soul as channel and mediator between the level of **TRUTH** (your Higher Self and Eternal Being) and the level of **REALITY**, which, as we will see, is not a "separate" level of the Truth, but rather a direct *result,* or, more precisely, an EXPRESSION or PRODUCT of the Truth.

So, we will now explore ENERGY through the ancient concept of the different levels of vibration and being, the so-called Depths of being, which were already used in ancient Tibet and China thousands of years ago.

# From the Nothing to the Spiritual Light of
# Truth and POTENTIAL
## The Universal Depths 9, 8, 7

*Anything has a source, except for source itself, since the source arises out of nothing . . .*

—Hermes Trismegistus, Hermeticum

*Energy is Vibration and Vibration is Life*! Understanding this principle will enable you to unlock the power of the universe!

So let us grasp this *vibration*, which we ourselves *are* with each breath and in each moment of our lives.

In ancient Far East Asian Philosophy, as we have heard before, the universe is seen as a unity of **9 Depths**, which are levels of vibration.

The **9th Depth** is the **"nothingness,"** the space before light and movement, before vibration, the level of utter darkness and stillness.

This "nothingness" contracts, and in doing so, it creates a *movement*, a *will to become and create*, and this initial movement is known as the 8th Depth. The number 8 has the form of a lemniscate, the eternal principal stated by Hermes Trismegistus "as above so below." The **8th Depth** is the **Source of all Sources**, out of which arises the spiritual light of 7th Depth, the level of ETERNAL BEING, the light and "food" for all creation!

Now, this **7th Depth**, or level, is where it becomes really interesting for you, since the spiritual light of 7th Depth is your **True Self.** It is your true home, the level of pure POTENTIAL, the source for our physical world, YOUR source for your reality!

## ANYTHING you do, create, and *are* in the physical world we live in has its origin in the spiritual light of 7th Depth.

Without the 7th Depth, the level governed by the **Sun**, NOTHING could exist; there would be no life, no light—you and our physical world would not exist.

It is the home of all creation, the level **above time and space**! It is the level of **enlightenment**, the **battery of life**, which in truth we always *are*, but which we tend to forget in our daily lives. It is man's—and in fact, all of creation's—task, to not only *reach* this level of enlightenment and POWER but to rather BE it at each and every moment in our lives.

*To be in 7th heaven*—as in the well-known proverb—means to consciously BE this spiritual light of creation, to BE the Source. *Being* the light of 7th Depth not only means owning and using the key to creation, but rather *being* CREATION and CREATOR at the same time, which among others means *being* total **HEALTH** and eternal **YOUTH**.

*Being* the light of 7th Depth means manifesting and *being* the Truth in your life.

*Being* TRUTH for **abundance, health,** and **happiness**

. . . but, in order to do this, the **Sun**, your Higher Self, needs the **Moon**, since without the Moon "potential" would always stay "potential" and would not be able to *realize* itself.

# The Individualization of Unity through the 6 Depths of Individual Being

*The Soul is a flame coming from God, the Lightning,*
*oh, should she not return to him?*

—Angelus Silesius

In order for the Truth to express itself, in order for the spiritual light of 7th Depth, the True and Higher Self, to become conscious of itself, it needs to individualize and manifest itself.

The **6th Depth** is the level of being where this *individualization* and incarnation begins. It is the **cosmic egg** that lies within the endless and eternal spiritual light of 7th Depth and which contains the raw energy of the 12 cosmic forces. The 6th Depth encompasses within itself Depths 5, 4, 3, 2, 1. It is the **womb of creation**, the matrix of physical existence. It is **Rhea**, the **Life Flow**, yearning to *realize* herself as form or physical *reality*.

In Greek mythology, **Rhea** is the daughter of heaven and Earth. She is the mother of the gods, who is married to her brother Kronos, the god of time.

Rhea, the **Life Flow**, is your **Soul** manifesting itself out of the spiritual light of 7th Depth by mediating between the Higher Self (heaven) and the body (the Earth).

The **6th Depth**, the cosmic egg, or Life Flow, is governed by the **Moon**, and just as your Soul mediates between the spiritual realms and the world of form (your body), so does the Moon mediate between the level of unity (heaven, 7th Depth) and the world of manifestation, which is our planet Earth, the "expression" and product of heaven.

The **Moon** is the **ruler of manifestation**, the ruler of the cosmic egg, the womb of creation. It is both the **Gate** to as well as the **Key** for the Sun/potential to express itself and for creation to unfold, and as such it is also *your* Key to create your own reality out of your Higher Self, your eternal light of Truth.

# The Moon is your Key to create your reality!

As shown on diagram number 1, the cosmic egg of creation is the zodiac with its 12 star signs, the 12 cosmic gates to Heaven and Earth. The zodiac is embedded within the endless and eternal golden spiritual light of 7th Depth and is waiting to unfold itself, like the petals of a flower, as the five-pointed star[1], Man's symbol of consciousness and health.

You, as the microcosm within the macrocosm, unfold yourself out of this cosmic egg of creation!

Your **Zodiac** is your **Life Flow**, your **Soul** creating her destiny and reality through her **12 Gates**, the Soul Gates. Diagram number 1 shows the Life Flow, Man's Microcosmic Orbit with the 6 Depths, each presented in the color of its element, since according to the five elements in Far-East Asian philosophy[2] each of the 6 Depths, or levels of being, relates to a specific element, which are (in the correct cosmic order of manifestation):

**Primordial Fire** (6th Depth, red)

**Quintessence** (Wood) (3rd Depth, green)

Air (Metal) (2nd Depth, white)

Earth (1st Depth, yellow)

**Fire** (5th Depth, red)

**Water** (4th Depth, blue)

The Primordial Fire of 6th Depth is not actually considered an element yet; it is the Fire (Matrix), which gives birth to the elements and out of which you unfold your potential as the five-pointed star of Man. These elements of the Depths are not to be confused with the 4 elements of the 12 star signs, the Gates of your Soul, lying within the Depths. If you look at Diagram number 1 you can see that out of each Depth arise two signs of the zodiac, which are the **Gates** of the Microcosmic (and the Macrocosmic) **Soul**. This means that each Depth gives birth to two cosmic, or Soul Forces, which in turn express themselves through an individual element, thus creating a unique and specific character out of these two elements.

As an example let us take a look at the **1st Depth**, which relates to the element Earth and is, therefore, shown in **Yellow**, the color representing the **Earth element**. As you can see on the Life Flow flowing centrally down the front and up the spine in the figure shown on the diagram, this Depth lies at the back of the neck between the 2nd thoracic vertebrae and the 1st cervical vertebrae. These two "points," or areas of the body, are the two **gates** lying within this Depth, mediating between the golden, spiritual light of 7th Depth, the *potential*, and the manifested level of incarnation, the body, and reality. They (or rather, your Soul) mediate between these two levels both through the element of the Depth (in this case the Earth element) as well as through their own unique element, which in this case is **Air** for the Gate of **Gemini** (2nd Thoracic vertebrae) and **Water** for the Gate of **Cancer** (1st Cervical vertebrae).

This shows us that, unlike what some people may think, the Eastern and Western element systems are not "separate" systems, but belong together and in fact are ONE and the SAME = the Soul, only expressing different levels of the Soul and the Universe. Considering only one level or element system (as is usually the case in either West or East) means denying one part of the Soul, and as such, denying your own Self.

This means that, in order to become "whole,"—in order to realize your full potential— you need to see the whole picture; you need to *think outside of the box*, or, to put it in different words, to behold your reality from *above*, from Source, from the level of potential, your own Self, looking *through* the Depths and your gates of your Soul *into* reality, which is the *product* of your mediation between the different levels of your Soul.

So, how does your **Soul** mediate between her **potential** (7th Depth / Source / spiritual plane) and her **"product"** (body level / form / reality)?

And what is the **Moon's** part in that?

Well, remember the key sentence of this book, and indeed, the Cosmic Code of Creation:

### *The Moon is for the Soul what the Soul is for you,*

which means: Just as the **Moon** travels through the zodiac on its monthly journey around our planet Earth and opens the 12 cosmic gates of the zodiac one by one, enabling the spiritual light of 7th Depth to manifest itself as physical existence, so does your Life Flow manifest itself through its 6 Depths and 12 Gates of the Soul, so does your **Soul,** in a continuous flow of light and energy, create her reality through the Depths of her Being and her 12 magical gates of creation—her gates of creation, which, as we will see in our next chapter, are not only the **gates** to your unlimited potential, but also at the same time your **keys** to fulfil your potential, since, as we will see and experience in detail in the practical part of this book, in cosmic creation . . .

### The Way is at the same time always the Goal!

# The 12 Soul Gates and the 12 Organ Flows to Create Your Reality!

| SUN | Spiritual light of 7th Depth **TRUTH** (Higher Self of Man) | |
| --- | --- | --- |
| MOON | **SOUL** | |
| EARTH | BODY | **Effect of Truth** Level of organ flows / Tools of the Soul |

(The diagram above shows the SOUL mediating between its Higher Self and the Body through its 12 Soul Gates, just like the MOON mediates between the Sun and Earth through the 12 Cosmic Gates of the Zodiac.)

The **Life Flow**, as we have learned in our last chapter, is your **Matrix**, your **energetic womb** out of which you create your reality. It is your **Soul**, your **personal source** arising out of the universal Source, the 7th Depth. The Life Flow contains within itself all Depths of incarnated being and thus all of your life's potential. It is your most important energy flow, flowing to the pubic bone from your navel (where the spark "enters" the body and the impulse is given), then up the spine, and again centrally down the body. Because of its importance, the Life Flow should be activated on a daily basis. This can easily be done by touching certain areas on your body in a specific sequence. At the beginning of the practical part of this book you will be shown in detail how to activate this most important Energy Flow of your body, but for now let us continue with the theory.

In order to manifest its energy and come into form and existence, the Life Flow needs **Gates** to pour the energy into reality and **Tools** to manifest itself and *create*. So what are these "Gates" and "Tools," and how do they function, or rather, how can your Soul, and thus YOU *use* them to create your reality?

In order to find out, let us have a look at the zodiac, and by "zodiac" I mean both the macrocosmic as well as the microcosmic **zodiac**, which is **YOU**. Whenever I refer to "cosmic terms," like "zodiac" or "cosmos" or "cosmic force," you should remember that whatever applies to the macrocosmic, or "large-scale" cosmos, also applies to the microcosmic version, you. YOU are the cosmos, which in its original Greek meaning means *order*, thereby already giving you a clue to what CREATION really is:

# Creation is order (cosmos)!

If you consciously want to create your own reality, it is imperative for you to understand and follow this order, which does NOT mean giving up your "identity," your uniqueness. On the contrary, following, or rather, *being* the cosmic order, as we will see is imperative to unfold your potential and allow your "uniqueness" to shine. The fact that the word "unique" contains in itself the syllable "uni," meaning "one" or "unity" is certainly no coincidence but rather a clue to what *being the cosmic order* really means:
using your ego rather than being controlled by it; it means rising above reality and form to the spiritual level of pure light and truth, rising to your true, Higher Self, to your unlimited potential.

*Being* the cosmic order means *becoming what you were born to BE,* and this is precisely why you need the 12 Gates and Tools of your Soul and what the **Moon** as the **Gatekeeper of these 12 Cosmic Gates** means for you.

So, let us have a look at the "Wheel of Life," both the Macrocosmic as well as the Microcosmic Zodiac, as shown on diagram number 1.

The **Zodiac**, or 6th Depth of Being, the Realm of the **Moon**, consists of 6 levels of being, 6 levels of vibration, with the 6th Depth being the Matrix that gives birth to the other five levels of incarnated being.

The Zodiac thus represents itself in a specific order (cosmos) of six color fields representing the elements and colors of the different Depths. Within these color fields lie the Cosmic Gates (Gates of the Soul), the signs of the Zodiac. Each sign (Gate) corresponds to, or rather, expresses itself *through* and *as* a specific Cosmic or **Organ Force,** which reveals their true meaning, since the word *organ* derives from the ancient Greek word *órganon*, the meaning of which is **Tool of the Soul.**

Thus, the Zodiac signs express themselves through the Organs of your body, which, as the ancient Greeks quite rightly knew, are much more than mere "lumps of cells" that keep us "alive" through their digestive and other body functions.

Your **Organs**, or, as we will see, your **Organ Flows**, are in fact your Tools to "build your body and your life." They are your **Tools to create your reality**, provided of course you understand how to use them.

## So, how do you use the Tools of your Soul, and what is an Organ Flow?

To understand what an Organ Flow is let's go back to the statement at the beginning of the book, that **Matter follows Energy.**

This is the answer, since your bodily organs, just like anything physical, are ALWAYS the product of a physically "invisible" energy, or "energy flow" behind it.

Hans-Peter Dürr, the famous German physicist and alternative Nobel prize winner, quite rightly said that . . .

> *Matter is only a structure of relations which, by becoming dense, seems as if it could be grasped,*

and this, as you will see and experience in detail in the second, practical part of this book, is precisely what cosmos (order) and creation, or rather, cosmic creation is all about, since

COSMIC CREATION IS THE MERGING OF ENERGIES IN A SPECIFIC ORDER.

It is the merging of energies and energy flows in an order given to us by COSMOS = ORDER itself, or rather, by the ruler of the cosmic egg of 6th Depth, the MOON.

By traveling through the 6 Depths of creation on its monthly journey around the Earth and *activating* the 12 cosmic forces **the moon is the Cosmic tone setter.** It "opens" the 12 Cosmic Gates of Creation and lets the whole Cosmos vibrate in the frequency corresponding to the gate the moon is currently opening.

Each cosmic gate resonates with a specific organ function energy in your body, which means that each of your organs, or tools of your body, has a unique vibration and energy flow "behind" it, which creates the physical organ—a vibration and a musical key, that corresponds to a specific sign of the Zodiac, and thus, to a specific cosmic gate or force.

The vibration or energy of your organs determines not only the state of individual organs, but also the state of your general health, which practically means:

**If the vibrations (the energy) of your organs resonate with their cosmic counterpart, then you are healthy, you feel great and are full of energy.**

If the vibrations (the energy) of your organs are "out of tune" with their cosmic counterpart, physical or emotional symptoms will occur.

Physical and/or emotional symptoms are the signals by which your Soul tries to convey to you the fact that your Soul melody is out of tune with the Moon, or rather, with the cosmic symphony of creation led by the Moon. Your Soul is demanding attention *through* the organ force and its associated characteristics, like for example the negative emotion of *fear*, which is associated with the kidney and bladder function arising out of 4th Depth. (You will learn and experience all the characteristics of the organ functions in detail in the practical part of the book in the following chapters). The negative emotion of *fear* thus is the voice of your Soul telling you that the vibration of your Kidney and/or Bladder Energy is "out of tune," or, to put it in other words, that there is a *blockage* within the respective energy flow.

**Energy or organ flows are streams of energy**, flowing through your body on specific pathways between the skin, muscles, and bones. In the practical part of this book you will find diagrams for each of the organ flows showing you the exact pathway through your body.

Organ flows, which in Traditional Chinese Medicine (TCM) are also known as "meridians," are the energy or "driving force" behind your physical organs, which means that your physical organs are the result of the respective organ flow behind it.

Any dis-ease in one or more of your organs is ALWAYS the result of one or more blockages in either the respective organ flow or/and another organ flow, since a blockage in one organ flow will disrupt the harmonious flow of other organ flows as well.

Your **12 organ flows**, each corresponding to a specific sign of the zodiac, aren't in fact 12 "separate streams," but rather one large energy flow, also known as the **large energy cycle**.

The large energy cycle is like a "factory" for the Life Flow (the Soul, or **Rhea** in Greek mythology) where its **reality** is created. It consists of **12** streams (the 12 sons of Rhea), which express the **4** elements of the Zodiac and form one large **energy flow or cycle.**[1] It arises out of the **Life Flow**, which is the energy flow that descends from **heaven**, or, as the bible puts it, from Eden.

*nd there sprang a river out of Eden to water the garden, and thence divided itself, and grew into four principal waters.*

—1st Book Moses, 2:10

Looking at the **large energy cycle** from a Trinity or Biblical point of view, this would be the level of the **12 Disciples** spreading the word of Jesus, the Life Flow, son of God (Heaven), thus realizing the **Holy Trinity**.

The 12 organ flows represent the 12 gates of the holy Jerusalem, *each of the 12 gates are made of a single pearl* (Revelation, 21:21) with the Pearl being not only the symbol for manifesting the truth (building your Holy Jerusalem), but also the symbol of the **Moon**, the key to your Higher Self, the truth and potential.

The 12 organ flows are the "precious stones" of the holy city (You!), each of them corresponding to a specific "stone," the symbol of manifestation.

They are your **most precious tools**, creating your reality and building, healing, cleansing, and regenerating your body in a continuous ascending and descending flow of energy—an Energy flow which you yourself are and which you can activate by simply following the Moon on its monthly journey, thus tuning yourself into the Cosmic Symphony of Creation.

In the following chapters, the "practical" part of this book, you will be shown how to activate your Life Flow according to the ancient Japanese healing art Jin Shin and how to daily tune the melody of your Soul into the cosmic vibration given to you by the Moon.

Following a short introduction, which includes the activation of the Life Flow, you will find six chapters, each dedicated to one cosmic Depth and its two cosmic or Soul forces.

You will get to know and use each of the **12 tools of your Soul** in detail and understand why certain foods and tastes have a healing effect on some days and not on others, why you feel happy and full of energy on some days, while on others your "energies" will be low (something you will be able to change by regularly tuning your body into the cosmic symphony of creation).

You will learn everything about the Soul Gates and what they mean for you, and you will discover in detail your organ forces, learn about their characteristics, and see their flowpaths through your body. Discovering the flowpaths of your organ flows will enable you to understand the connections of certain body parts to specific organs, like for example the eyes to the liver. You will understand why harmonizing your liver energy will, for example, not only heal your liver, but at the same time improve your eyesight, make your body more flexible, and prevent cancer.

Studying and applying the cosmic wisdom shown in the practical part of this book, will enable you to master the 12 Soul forces and become master of your own destiny.

This will enable you to **heal** and **create** your own **reality** in tune with the cosmic symphony of creation led by the creative principle of your Soul , the

## MOON!

# How to Activate the Code of Creation

The **Moon**, as we have learned, is the ruler of 6th Depth, the Zodiac or cosmic egg, the matrix of creation.

As such, the Moon is not only the cosmic tone setter, but also, and most importantly for you, it is YOUR very personal tone setter and guide to total Health and Wellbeing.

To *be* healthy, happy, and successful means to be *in tune* with the Moon, and this is precisely what the next chapters of this book will be about.

They will take you on a journey through the 6 Depths of your being and the 12 gates of your Soul .

It is the journey of your LIFE, since LIFE is VIBRATION and the Moon's journey through the 12 cosmic gates of creation *is* vibration.

It is a journey through the 6 cosmic energy "fields" and their corresponding elements, enabling these energies and vibrations to merge together in a specific order (cosmos), thus creating EARTH out of HEAVEN in a continuous ascending and descending flow of energy, an energy which is . . .

## YOU!

The following six chapters will take you on the journey of the Moon. Each chapter is dedicated to one Depth of being and its two star signs, the gates to heaven, explained through their respective organ forces, the **tools of your Soul** .

Every day, the Moon, by its position in the zodiac, will provide you with the **key energy** to your Higher Self, thus enabling you to open that particular gate of your Soul which corresponds to the Moon's position in the zodiac. By activating the corresponding organ function energy, you will rise above reality and become a channel for the pure Light of 7th Depth, the unlimited potential, which is pure **health** and **eternal youth**. Your life will undergo a magical transformation, enabling you to **heal** and **rejuvenate** and BE the FLOW which cosmic creation is all about.

In order to activate your **organ functions, the tools of your Soul** , you will work with 26 energy locks on your body as shown on diagram number 9. Energy locks are "points" or "areas" on your body by which you can access your organ flows, thus removing blockages and harmonizing the flow of energy.

Each organ function (tool of your Soul ) is activated by a specific energy lock combination. This means: In order to activate an organ function you simply touch the energy locks with your hands as shown both in writing as well as on photographs in the corresponding chapter.

"Touching"—and thus *opening*—your energy locks does not involve any pressure or massaging nor is there any need to take off your clothes.

Activating your organ flows, as you will see and experience in six chapters of the moon's journey, is simple and extremely effective and will supply your whole being with vital energy.
However, before we start our journey through the 6 Depths of being and the 12 gates of your Soul in order to activate the code of creation, I want to show you how to activate your **Life Flow**, since the Life Flow, as explained in the past chapters, is the **matrix** from which you create your reality. It is your **personal source** that feeds your organ flows, and as such it should be activated and cared for on a daily basis. Activating your **Life Flow** will support all your **organ flows**, and activating your organ flows will in turn support your Life Flow, since it is all about the continuous flow of life energy, the continuous transformational process of your . . .

# SOUL!

# Activating Your Life Flow, Your Personal Source

Activating your Life Flow is a similar procedure to activating your organ flows, since your hands and fingers are all you need to "get your energy flowing." The Life Flow is a sequence of eight "steps" that can be done at any time. Personally, I like to activate the Life Flow either first thing in the morning, or before going to sleep in the evening. The Life Flow will always give you exactly what you need. In the morning it will **energize you** so you can excel at whatever you will do during the day, and in the evening it will **calm you** and thus help you to fall asleep. The Life Flow strengthens your **nerves**, harmonizes your **glands** and **hormones**, activates your **immune system,** and **rejuvenates** your whole being. It acts as a whole, but the eight steps also unfold individual effects, as explained in the Life Flow activation sequence.

To activate your Life Flow, have a look at the diagram shown on page 24 ("Life Flow Sequence"). The green points on the figure are the areas where you will place your hands. On each step you should stay about 3 minutes or until you feel the energy pulsating under your fingers.

One thing that I would like to point out before discussing the eight steps of the Life Flow is the important part that your breath plays in the activation of energy and energy flows in general. This is why you should breathe consciously and become AWARE of your BREATH. When you activate your Life Flow, imagine the energy moving UP the spine and centrally DOWN the front of your body in an endless circle. Inhaling deeply and consciously will support the energy's flow, spine upwards, whereas exhaling aids the flow of energy down the front of your body.

# Life Flow Activation Sequence

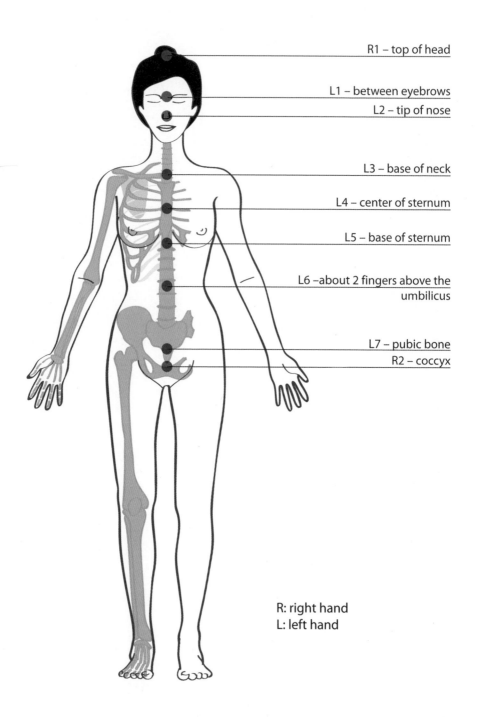

R1 – top of head

L1 – between eyebrows
L2 – tip of nose

L3 – base of neck

L4 – center of sternum

L5 – base of sternum

L6 –about 2 fingers above the umbilicus

L7 – pubic bone
R2 – coccyx

R: right hand
L: left hand

# Simply BE THE FLOW with both your hands as well as with your BREATH!

Here is how to activate the Life Flow:

**First step:**
Place the fingers (or the palm) of your right hand on **top of your head** while placing the fingers of your left hand **between your eyebrows** (Third Eye).

This step aids all mental processes and increases memory. It regulates the blood pressure, energizes the nerves, and promotes a healthy, youthful appearance. Furthermore, this step helps both the physical as well as the spiritual eye-sight.

**Second step:**
Your right hand stays on top of your head while you place the fingers of your left hand on the **tip of your nose**.

This step aids and harmonizes the reproductive organs. It aids the superficial body energy as well as the eyes and "opens" up the middle of the body.

**Third step:**
Your right hand stays on top of your head while your left hand wanders to the little hollow at the **upper end of your sternum** (breast bone) with your fingers pointing downwards if possible.

This step aids the assimilation of calcium and increases mental balance. It activates the thyroid gland, activates the metabolism, and supports anything to do with expression and communication.

**Fourth step:**
The right hand stays on top of your head while you place your left hand (or the fingers of your left hand) on the **center of your sternum**.

Here you are actually touching your Heart Chakra, the main energy center for emotions. This step harmonizes your emotions and helps your heart and your lungs. It prevents breast cancer and generally increases your immune system since it activates the thymus gland. This step is like a tonic to be happy! If you are feeling down and do not have the time to activate the whole flow, simply do this step for a couple of minutes and feel your worries disappear!

**Fifth step:**

Your right hand stays on top of your head while with your left hand you touch the area **just below your sternum**.

This step "opens" the Solar plexus, which is like a crossroads for all energy flows in the human body. This step activates your kidney, spleen, and heart functions, harmonizes the nervous and the immune system, and balances negative emotions such as hate or jealousy.

**Sixth step:**

Again, your right hand stays on top of your head while you place the fingers of your left hand about **an inch above your navel**.

With this step you touch the Sagittarius Soul Gate, which is located at the umbilicus and through which the spark of creation "enters" your body to become the Microcosmic Orbit. Visualizing this spark, which you yourself *are*, helps in identifying yourself with your inner Self rather than with your appearance or Ego. This step supplies you with vital life energy and fills you with harmony and inner joy.

**Seventh step:**

Your right hand is still on top of your head while your left hand wanders to your pubic bone.

This step pulls the energy from your head down the front of your body, thus helping your energy to move up the spine again. It clears your head, strengthens the spine, and gives physical stability. This step also activates the reproductive organs and activates the metabolism.

**Eighth step:**

With this step it is your left hand that stays on the pubic bone, while your right hand wanders to the **coccyx** (base of spine).

This—last—step of our Life Flow sequence "opens" the pelvis and aids the energy flow into and out of the legs. It warms hands and feet and aids the reproductive organs.

# Quickie to Activate Your Life Flow

If you do not have enough time to do the whole flow sequence of the Life Flow, there is a simple—yet highly effective—quick method to get your personal source flowing and energize your whole being.

Simply touch the palm of one hand with the fingers of your other hand as shown in the photograph. You may either do it with one hand, or—ideally—touch one hand for a few minutes (three minutes or longer) and then the other hand.

The simple act of touching the base of your palm for a couple of minutes as shown in the photograph on the left will energize your whole being, get yourself centered, and make you feel absolutely splendid!

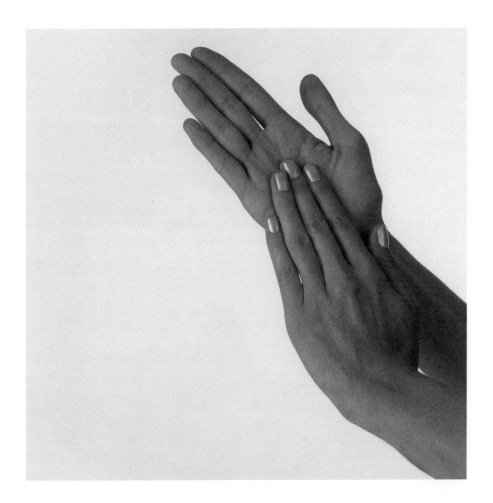

# Unfolding Your **STAR** with the **MOON** and What It Means to Be *In Tune!*

The following six chapters are your personal journey with the Moon through the Depths of your Soul .

It is the most intimate journey of your life—the journey to your inner SELF—to what you really *are*, or rather, what you were born to BE!

By following the Moon and tuning into its changing vibrations, you will be unfolding your five-pointed star, or rather, you will be unfolding yourself *as* the five-pointed star you were born to BE.

Each Depth gives you specific lessons to be learned and traits to develop. When you have been following the moon through your personal Depths over a longer period of time you will notice that there are certain Depths (certain days in the month) where you tend to feel more emotional, get upset easier, etc.

Often these Depths are related to your personal horoscope, specifically to your sun sign, the rising star as well as the moon sign.

For example: People born under the sign of Libra often get either more tired (or are actually feeling better) during days when the Moon is either traveling through the sign of Libra or its opposing sign Aries.[1]

This is a sign that these Depths and their organ functions need specific attention. A way to give that attention would be to hold the respective finger (shown in each chapter) a bit longer and more often than the fingers on the other days.

Each Depth represents a point of your star with the sixth Depth being the source as the center of the star.

You unfold the star, *your potential,* by unlocking the gates of your Soul  in tune with the moon.

All you need for this are your fingers and your breath—lightly place your hands or fingers on specific areas (energy locks) as shown in each chapter under the heading

"Activating the . . . energy." It will show you both in writing as well as with a photograph where to place your hands to activate the respective energy flow. As you will see, we always use both hands to establish a flow of energy between two poles or energy locks, which will then jump-start and activate the whole organ flow. Let your breath flow freely and allow your energy to "do the work for you"!

You will open your Soul gates by activating the respective organ function. The organ function given to you by the position of the moon is your daily key and tool to open the respective gate and play the melody of your Soul in tune with the cosmic symphony of creation led by the Moon.

In order to tune yourself into the cosmic vibration, it is essential for you to know the position of the Moon within the zodiac. One way to find this out is by going onto my webpage (irenelauretti.com) where you will find the current star sign activated by the Moon.

When you know the position of the Moon, simply go to the relevant chapter where you will not only find all the necessary information for tuning yourself into the cosmic vibration, but also lots of other useful information about certain foods and flavors that will enhance your harmony with the cosmic vibration, physical exercises you should or should not do on certain days, as well as all the information about the relevant Soul gate and the organ flow with its flowpath through the body.

On its monthly journey around the Earth the Moon stays in each sign / cosmic gate for about two to three days. During this time the whole cosmos vibrates in the vibration of this specific sign. If you could hear this with your physical ears, you would hear the cosmic symphony of creation in a specific musical key. By activating the corresponding organ function you tune the melody of your Soul into the cosmic symphony of creation and play your unique Soul melody in tune with the whole of cosmos.

## Being *in tune* means to be healthy, full of energy, and in a great mood!

The more regularly and consistently you tune yourself into the cosmic vibration given by the Moon, the better you will feel. When the energy flows start flowing freely again, they will clear blockages, which may have affected you for many years. This cleansing process will sometimes bring up old and long-forgotten traumas and even physical symptoms. This is a natural and normal reaction of your body shedding itself of "negative" energy and removing blockages. When these natural healing reactions occur it is important that you continue with your daily activation sequences and drink lots of water and/or herbal teas to support the cleansing of your body.

Visualizing your Self as LIGHT . . . and your body transforming, renewing itself out of this light—which it is actually doing through the process of tuning-in—may enhance the transformative process of activating the code and unfolding your six Depths of being, your personal star!

And, since activating the Code by tuning yourself into the Moon's vibration is never "just" about your body, but rather about transforming your whole reality, it is also advisable for you to imagine the reality you would like to create for yourself, since— as you will see and experience in our next chapters . . .

### YOU yourself are the CREATOR
### and the KEY to your own REALITY!

# Microcosmic orbit (human) within the Macrocosmic Orbit (Zodiac)
## The Life Flow and the Soul Gates of Man

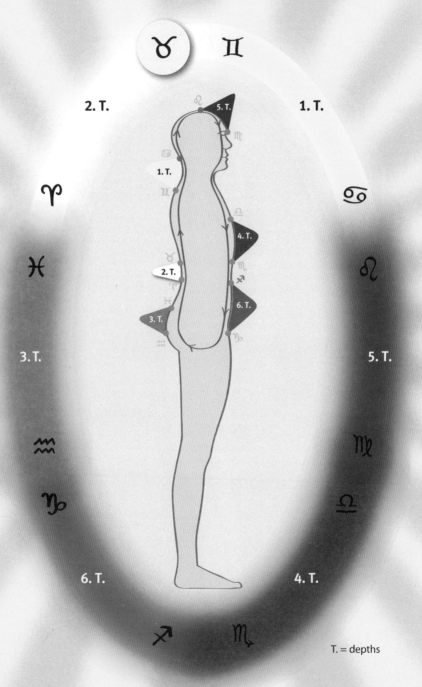

# The Life Flow/Microcosmic Orbit

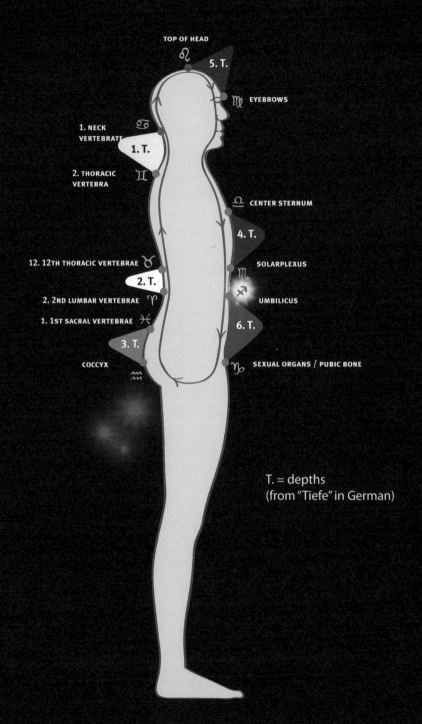

TOP OF HEAD

5. T.

EYEBROWS

1. NECK VERTEBRATE

1. T.

2. THORACIC VERTEBRA

CENTER STERNUM

4. T.

12. 12TH THORACIC VERTEBRAE

SOLARPLEXUS

2. T.

2. 2ND LUMBAR VERTEBRAE

UMBILICUS

1. 1ST SACRAL VERTEBRAE

6. T.

3. T.

COCCYX

SEXUAL ORGANS / PUBIC BONE

T. = depths
(from "Tiefe" in German)

# The Five-Pointed Star

9. T.

8. T.

7. T.

6. T.

T = Depths

Ascending flow
Descending flow

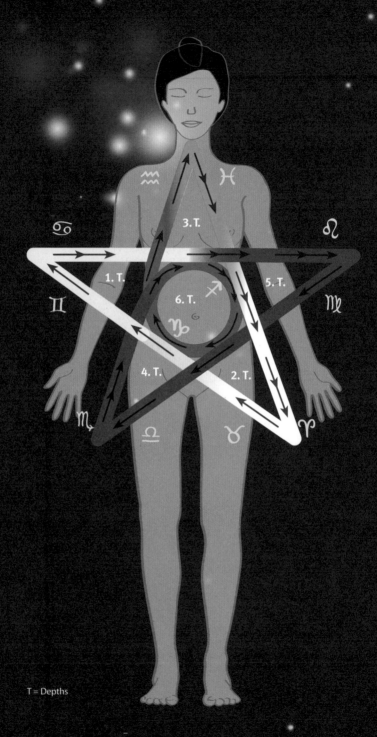

# The Unfolding of The Star through 4 Golden Triangles

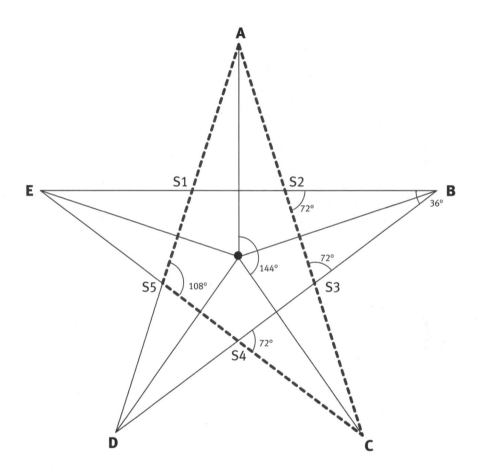

The dotted lines show the first of the four obtuse-angled golden triangles within one cycle of creation. Each moon-cycle of creation creates 4 golden triangles (3) to unfold the five-pointed star, opening the 12 Soul/cosmic gates, thus revealing the Cosmic Code of Creation: 3x4=12!

# TABLE I

The 6 Cosmic Soul Depths and Their 12 Cosmic Forces (Gates)
with Their Organ Correspondences

| Depth Planetary Level | Star Sign Element Zodiac | Organ Flow Tool | Star sign Element Zodiac | Organ Flow Tool |
|---|---|---|---|---|
| 6th Depth Primordial Fire | ♐ Sagittarius Fire | Diaphragm | ♑ Capricorn Earth | Umbilicus |
| 3rd Depth Quintessence | ♒ Aquarius Air | Gallbladder | ♓ Pisces Water | Liver |
| 2nd Depth Air (Metal) | ♈ Aries Fire | Lungs | ♉ Taurus Earth | Large Intestine |
| 1st Depth Earth | ♊ Gemini Air | Stomach | ♋ Cancer Water | Spleen |
| 5th Depth Fire | ♌ Leo Fire | Heart | ♍ Virgo Earth | Small Intestine |
| 4th Depth Water | ♎ Libra Air | Bladder | ♏ Scorpio Water | Kidney |

# TABLE II

| Cosmic force | | Depth | Organ flow | Musical key | Day time | Age |
|---|---|---|---|---|---|---|
| Capricorn | ♑ | 6 | Umbilicus | G Major | 22.00 – 24.00 | 0–3 |
| Wassermann | ♒ | 3 | Gallbladder | A Major | 24.00 – 02.00 | 4–5 |
| Pisces | ♓ | 3 | Liver | B-sharp Major | 02.00 – 04.00 | 6–8 |
| Aries | ♈ | 2 | Lungs | D-flat Major | 04.00 – 06.00 | 9–13 |
| Taurus | ♉ | 2 | Large intestine | E-flat Major | 06.00 – 08.00 | 11–13 |
| Gemini | ♓ | 1 | Stomach | F-sharp Major | 08.00 – 10.00 | 14–16 |
| Cancer | ♋ | 1 | Spleen | G-sharp Major | 10.00 – 12.00 | 17–24 |
| Leo | ♌ | 5 | Heart | A-sharp Major | 12.00 – 14.00 | 25–32 |
| Virgo | ♍ | 5 | Small intestine | C Major | 14.00 – 16.00 | 33–40 |
| Libra | ♎ | 4 | Bladder | D Major | 16.00 – 18.00 | 41–48 |
| Scorpio | ♏ | 4 | Kidney | E Major | 18.00 – 20.00 | 49–56 |
| Sagittarius | ♐ | 6 | Diaphragm | F Major | 20.00 – 22.00 | 57–64 |

Capricorn's umbilicus section represents the time of the foetus in the womb, birth, and the first three years in life, which is why this energy is often referred to as "the first step" of creation. However, it is Sagittarius umbilicus function energy that completes a cycle and in doing so at the same time acts as the initiator for the new cycle, hence the location of the Sagittarius Soul gate at the navel.

# The 12 Organ Flows of the Large Energy Cycle and Their Division into the 4 Cosmic Elements

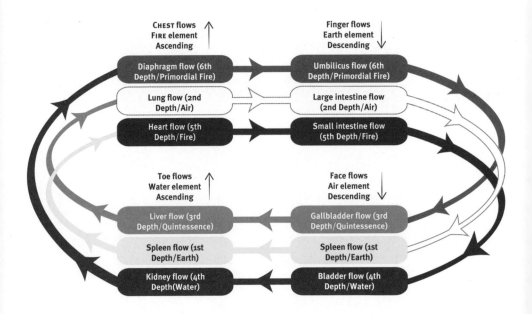

| | |
|---|---|
| **Chest flows**<br>**Fire element**<br>Ascending ↑ | **Finger flows**<br>Earth element<br>Descending ↓ |
| Diaphragm flow (6th Depth/Primordial Fire) | Umbilicus flow (6th Depth/Primordial Fire) |
| Lung flow (2nd Depth/Air) | Large intestine flow (2nd Depth/Air) |
| Heart flow (5th Depth/Fire) | Small intestine flow (5th Depth/Fire) |
| **Toe flows**<br>**Water element**<br>Ascending ↑ | **Face flows**<br>Air element<br>Descending ↓ |
| Liver flow (3rd Depth/Quintessence) | Gallbladder flow (3rd Depth/Quintessence) |
| Spleen flow (1st Depth/Earth) | Spleen flow (1st Depth/Earth) |
| Kidney flow (4th Depth(Water) | Bladder flow (4th Depth/Water) |

| | |
|---|---|
| **Chest-Fire flows** | ↑ : vital Source of life, Fire, pure flame of Spirit |
| **Finger-Earth flow** | ↓ : reproduction, renewal, digestion, unconditional cosmic Love |
| **Toe-Water flows** | ↑ : for critical conditions, highly energizing |
| **Face-Air flows** | ↓ : mental needs, forces of the mind |

# The Finger, Elements and Emotions

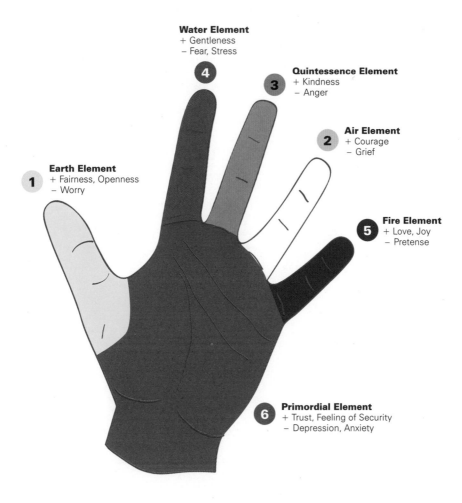

**Water Element**
+ Gentleness
– Fear, Stress

**Quintessence Element**
+ Kindness
– Anger

**Air Element**
+ Courage
– Grief

**Earth Element**
+ Fairness, Openness
– Worry

**Fire Element**
+ Love, Joy
– Pretense

**Primordial Element**
+ Trust, Feeling of Security
– Depression, Anxiety

+ Positive Emotion
– Negative Emotion

# The Cross of the 4 Elements

The Take-over-points for the organ flows, where the organ flows merge into their subsequent flows form the cross of man. Keeping your organ flows in harmony by tuning into the moon on a regular basis means mastering the cross of man, which means to master life and to consciously BE the CREATOR of your REALITY!

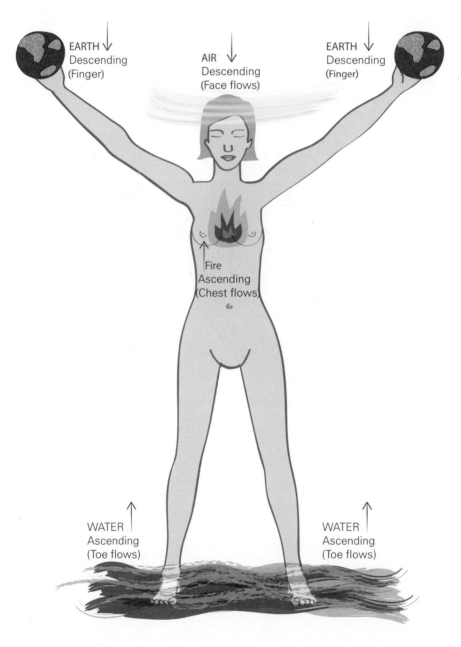

# TABLE III
Meaning and Positions of the 26 Energy Locks of MAN

| Energy Lock (EL) | Position | Meaning |
|---|---|---|
| 1 | Inside of the knee | Prime Mover |
| 1a | A hand above EL 1 | |
| 2 | Upper edge of hip bone | Wisdom, Life Force |
| 3 | Upper back, the inside and upper corners of the shoulder blades | Door |
| 4 | Base of skull, at the occipital ridge | Window to Consciousness |
| 5 | Inside of the ankle, between the ankle bone and the heel | Transformation |
| 6 | On the arch of the foot, about midway between the sole side of the big toe and the end of the heel | Balance, Discrimination |
| 7 | Tip of the big toe | Victory |
| 8 | Lateral side of the back of the knee | Rhythm, Strength; as Above, so Below |
| 8a | A hand above EL 8 | |
| 9 | Bottom of the shoulder blades, towards the spine | Ending of One Cycle, Beginning of another |
| 10 | Medium, inner edge of shoulder blade | Abundance |
| 11 | Angle between neck and shoulder | Releasing the Past |

| 12 | Midway between skull and shoulders, left and right to cervical vertebra number 4 | Not my Will (ego), but Thy Will (Higher Self) |
|---|---|---|
| 13 | On the front of the rib cage, by the third rib | Love Thy Enemies |
| 14 | On the front bottom of the rib cage | Equilibrium |
| 15 | In the groin | Happiness |
| 16 | On the outside of the ankle, between the ankle bone and the heel | Breaking down of existing forms in Favor of New Ones |
| 17 | Outside of the wrists, on the little-finger side | Relaxation of nerves |
| 18 | Palm side of the base of the thumb | Body Consciousness |
| 19 | Crease of the elbows, on the thumb side | Authority |
| 19a | A hand above EL 19 | |
| 20 | Above the eyebrow | Eternity |
| 21 | Underside of cheekbones | Escape from Mental Bondage |
| 22 | Under the collarbones | Complete Adaptation |
| 23 | On the back, under the costal arch | Controller of Human Destiny |
| 24 | Outer top of the foot, about midway between the little toe and the ring toe | Harmonizing Chaos |
| 25 | On the sit-bones | Quietly Regenerating |
| 26 | Outer edge of the shoulder blades near the armpit | Complete; That which was, is, and will be |

# The 26 Energy Locks

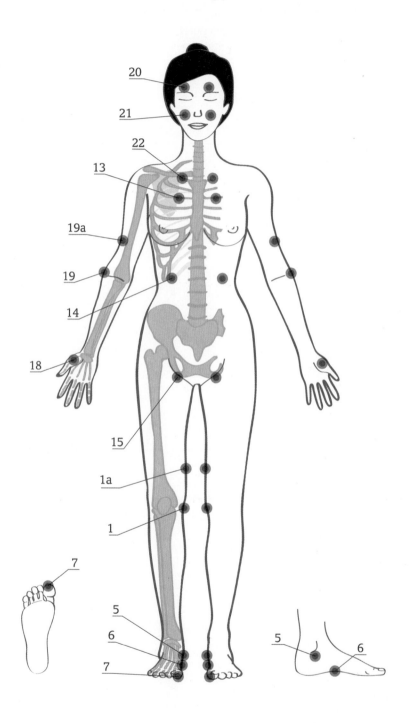

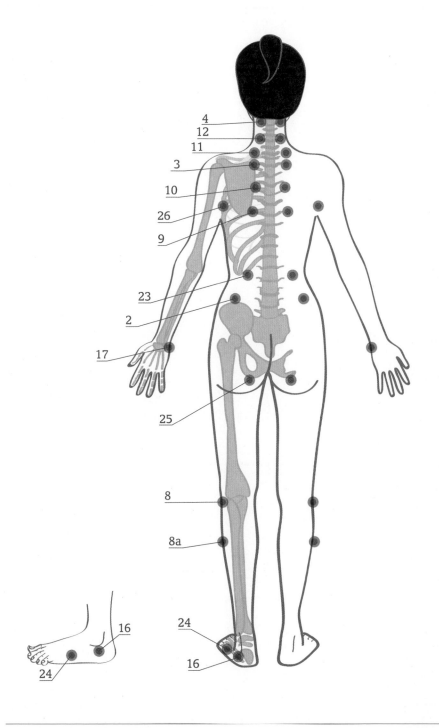

# Unfolding Your **STAR** for
# **HEALTH, HAPPINESS** and **SUCCESS!**

Your personal journey
through the depths of your being!

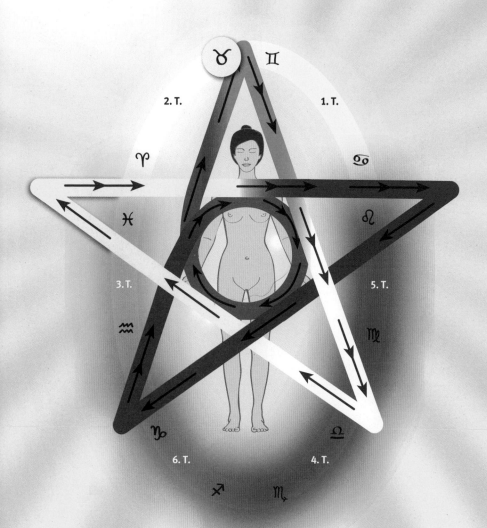

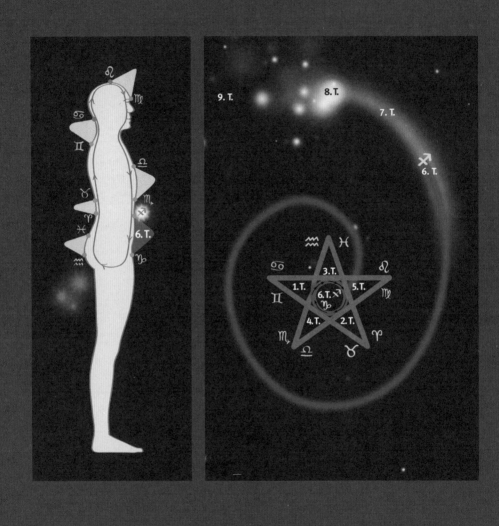

# 6th Depth—Spiraling Circle
## Primordial Fire

The MOON Travels through the 6th Depth
and Opens the Cosmic Gate of SAGITTARIUS Followed
by the Cosmic Gate of CAPRICORN

For you this means that you begin the dance of your Soul 's
12 creative forces by opening your . . .

### SAGITTARIUS Soul Gate *through* the Vibration of Diaphragm Function Energy,

followed by your . . .

### CAPRICORN Soul Gate *through* the Vibration of Umbilicus Function Energy!

# The Primordial Fire of the 6th Depth
## Your Personal Source

"The 6th Depth is your cosmic
egg of creation—it is your Soul."

—Irene Lauretti

The 6th Depth follows the spiritual light of the 7th Depth. It is the vibrational level where "incarnation" and manifestation into form begins. 6th Depth is ruled by the MOON, which is why the Moon is the ruler of creation as such. Without the 6th Depth there would be no creation, there would be no physical world, and unity would not be able to experience itself as diversity.

6th Depth is the cosmic egg of creation, which encompasses in itself the 12 signs of the zodiac and all levels (Depths) of incarnation.

It is the mediator between the 7th Depth, kingdom of the SUN and the EARTH, the product of the MOON's merging of the cosmic energies on his monthly journey . . .

The sixth Depth is your personal "egg of creation."

7th Depth is unity, is one-ness. The moment this ONE-ness wants to become conscious of itSELF, it needs to experience diversity, or, to put it in other words, it needs to experience "borders" and confinement.

Anything within the zodiac is "confined," or rather, experiences itself as "being confined." The moment the idea, the spark, enters the zodiac, it enters the level of "time" and mortality. It still IS oneness and eternal life, but the confines of the zodiac, the Soul 's very own tools and keys for eternal life, need to be opened consciously, which is precisely what you are doing by tuning into the moon as described in this and the following chapters.

The 6th Depth (the light red area on the zodiac) with its gates of Sagittarius and Capricorn is your "gate of entry" into the world of manifestation.

The moment the Moon reaches the Sagittarius Gate, which is the first gate of the 6th Depth, there is a **new beginning** both in nature as well as in your personal life. After its descending journey (gates of Gemini to Scorpio) the moon starts to ascend again with the entry into the gate of Sagittarius. (The monthly ascending and descending of the moon is not to be confused with the monthly waxing and waning of the moon!)

**Sagittarius** is the **impulse** to a new cycle of creation through the 12 Cosmic Gates. It is the spark of 7th Depth, the idea striving for manifestation through the 12 gates of creation.

The 6th Depth is the **Big Breath of Life**. It is your primordial fire, your **personal source** pouring out of the spiritual light of the 7th Depth, giving birth to the 5 elements, which for you means:

By tuning into the 6th Depth through the diaphragm flow (Sagittarius), followed by the umbilicus flow (Capricorn), you become ONE with the big Breath of Life through which you are constantly connected to all living beings and to the whole universe.

Tuning into the 6th Depth harmonizes **relationships** and fills you with **warmth**. It extends your perspective and enables you to see from a more universal perspective.

The 6th Depth is known as the main harmonizer and healer of **autoimmune diseases** and restores the **will to live** in those who have lost it due to traumatic experiences and depression. It alleviates and **heals fatigue** and **exhaustion**.

**Tuning into the vibration of 6th Depth is like drinking from a well of pure light and energy, which is why 6th Depth is also known as the cosmic "charging station" for your daily life.**

It is the **core** of the five-pointed star of Man, which you are unfolding by tuning into the vibration of the moon as described in these practical chapters.

Here is a quick and easy way to harmonize the vibration of 6th Depth and connect yourself to SOURCE for an immediate increase in **energy** and **vitality** and a feeling of "total security" and harmony:

# Connecting to SOURCE
## Palm of Hands

The "quickie method" of harmonizing the 6th Depth, your personal source, as you may remember, is also the short version to activate the Life Flow, which of course IS the 6th Depth. This means that by touching the palm of your hand you activate your Life Flow and harmonize the Core of your physical existence.

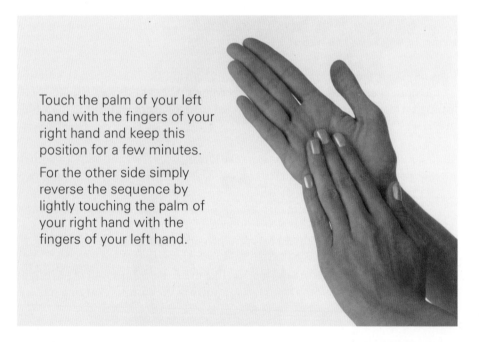

Touch the palm of your left hand with the fingers of your right hand and keep this position for a few minutes.

For the other side simply reverse the sequence by lightly touching the palm of your right hand with the fingers of your left hand.

My suggestion: If you can only use one hand, simply fold your fingers so that the fingertips touch the palm. This is completely unobtrusive and will give you a quick and powerful energy boost whilst calming stressed nerves at the same time!

There is no coincidence that prayers are done folding the hands or laying them together. When you pray you touch the palm of your hand, your personal source, and this is exactly what it is about—the connection to YOUR SOURCE of energy, wisdom, and light!

# General Tips for the Moon's Journey through the 6th Depth

- When the moon travels through the gates of Sagittarius and Capricorn you don't need as much sleep as for example during the Moon's journey through 4th Depth (Virgo and Scorpio). In fact, lying in too late may rob you of energy rather than supply you with energy. Rather, you should set your alarm clock to an hour earlier, and start the day by activating the Life Flow, which belongs to 6th Depths and is the matrix of your being, the source for all your activities!

- **Food:** As an all-encompassing Depth, the 6th Depth—contrary to the Depths 5, 4, 3, 2, 1—does not have any particular food or taste correspondences. However, since the ruler of the 6th Depth is the moon, my suggestion would be to favor **rice** as a grain during the days of the moon's journey through the 6th Depth. According to ancient Indian cosmology, rice is the food of the Moon that not only enhances your health and wellbeing but that will also increase your wealth, if eaten with the appropriate visualization and thoughts!

## Rice is the grain of the Moon!

- **Color: Red**—is the color of the 6th Depth. It has a highly vitalizing effect, mostly on the sexual organs, which—as you can see on the diagram on page 31—have a close relation to the 6th Depth since they are located in the part of body that corresponds to the 6th Depth. Visualizing this color may increase your harmony with the Moon during its journey through the Gates of Sagittarius and Capricorn and help to activate your reproductive organs, increasing fertility and the desire to make love. Most sexual problems have their root in this Depth, and in particular in the disharmony of the Umbilicus function energy, which—as we will see—is the Key to the Capricorn Soul Gate, the second gate within this Depth.

# 6th Depth and Emotional Growth

On the emotional level, which is the "mirror" of our Soul, the same principle as already mentioned above applies, since the 6th Depth is an all-encompassing Depth that does not correspond to any particular emotion. However, since a disharmony in this energy field may show up as utter despair and suicidal thoughts, tuning into the 6th Depth will reward you with

## TOTAL EQUILIBRIUM and the feeling of SECURITY and UNITY with all beings of the universe.

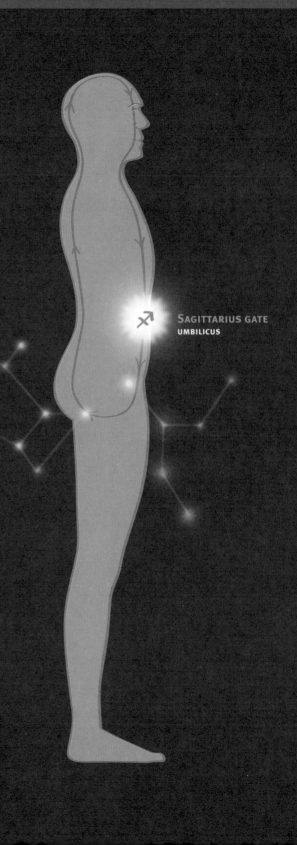

SAGITTARIUS GATE
UMBILICUS

# THE MOON OPENS THE COSMIC GATE OF
# **SAGITTARIUS**

*You Open Your Sagittarius Soul Gate through the*
*Vibration of Diaphragm Function Energy*

**Sagittarius** says:
**"I PERCEIVE**; I can perceive the TRUTH of the
7th Depth through the 6th Depth."

When the Moon enters and opens the cosmic gate of **Sagittarius**, the **diaphragm function energy** is your key to be in tune with the cosmic symphony of creation. It is your unique key to be healthy and deliver the highest performance in whatever you want to achieve during the Sagittarius days.

If you could physically "hear" the cosmic symphony of creation on a Sagittarius day, it would sound in **F Major**. Tuning yourself into this cosmic vibration by activating the diaphragm function energy (as shown below) will let the melody of your Soul— and thus YOU!—vibrate in the same vibration as Cosmos and reward you with the positive attributes associated with this musical key, such as **self-confidence** and **charisma.** F Major is said to have a **stabilizing** and **grounding** effect on highly sensitive persons with a vivid imagination, which means that activating your diaphragm flow will enable you to deliver your truth—which is your SELF—into the world.

Let us now have a look at the Sagittarius Soul gate, which we open by activating the diaphragm function energy, and which is located, as shown in diagram number 1, at the umbilicus and thus in the center of the human body, just like the 6th Depth, the mother-Depth of the diaphragm function energy, forms the **center** of the five-pointed star about to unfold (see diagram number 3 "The five-pointed star") . . .

. . . the center or the dormant core, from which you unfold your potential, which means:

The **Sagittarius Soul gate** at the **umbilicus** as the first gate within the light red part of the zodiac, the 6th Depth, corresponds to the area in which the divine spark, the essence of breath, receives the impulse to become physical form and where the individualization and unfolding as five-pointed star begins.

By activating the diaphragm function energy you conduct the essence of breath through the navel into your body, so that the dance of creation, the dance of the divine spark through the **12 forces of creation** may begin.

This major significance of the navel area as the **beginning** and—as we will later see—also as the **completion** of the dance of creation, the unfolding of the five-pointed star, is no doubt the reason why the energies of all organs and glands, of the brain and the nervous system merge together in the navel area and can in fact be harmonized by activating the Diaphragm Function Energy, which we will now have a closer look at.

The diaphragm function energy is an ascending chest flow[1], which means that it flows in an **ascending** movement from the chest to the ring finger.[2] It is also known as a so-called "double Fire-flow" since it manifests the primordial Fire of 6th Depth *through* the Fire element of Sagittarius, which in practical terms means that this flow—similar to the Heart Flow of Leo—is all about FIRE and LOVE.

Activating your Sagittarius energy fills your heart with **vital life energy**. It increases your **physical** and **mental flexibility** from its core and has a preventive as well as a healing effect for the heart, which is why the Diaphragm function energy (DFE) is also known as the most important **heart-protection flow** which can in fact prevent heart attacks.

The diaphragm function energy, however, not only fills your heart with spiritual fire, but also has a **cooling effect** and will thus help you "cool down" if you are feeling too hot. This is the reason why people with a hot, quick-tempered and extrovert personality, which is likely to be more obvious on Sagittarius days than during the days when the moon travels through the other cosmic gates, will particularly benefit from the activation of this flow.

To sum up, we can say that the diaphragm function energy has an invigorating and strengthening effect that will energize and activate the **immune system** and the **sexual energy** as well as protect your heart.

# Flowpath of Sagittarius Energy

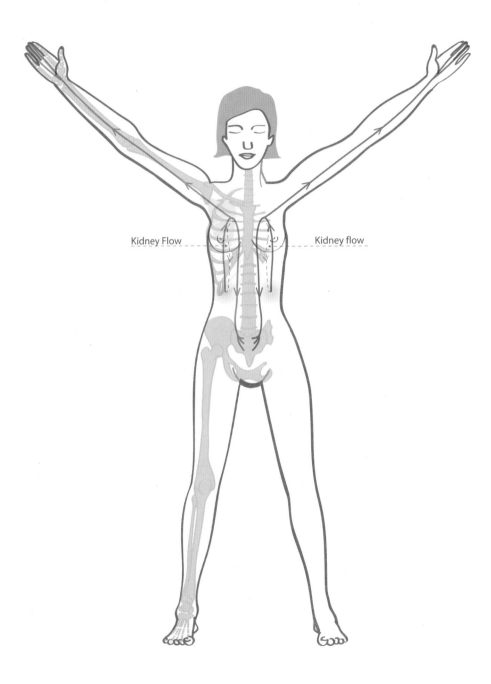

Kidney Flow _ _ _ _ _ _ _ _ _ _ _ Kidney flow

# HOW TO ACTIVATE THE ORGAN FLOWS
## Activating the Diaphragm Function Energy

Activating your diaphragm function energy—and the organ flows in general—is simple. All you need is your hands and fingers to place on specific points (energy locks) on your body as shown in the photographs.

You find the diagram with the complete list of energy locks on pages 42–45.

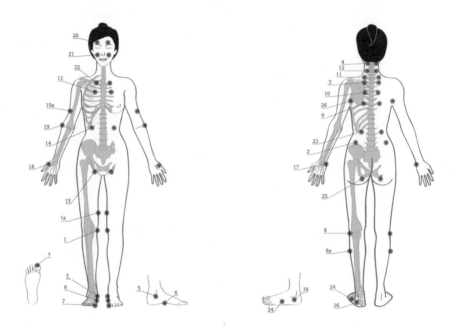

Each energy lock has a unique meaning, a specific vibration, just as the whole energy flow you are activating has a unique vibration, a specific musical key, etc.

For the activation of the energy flows as such it is not imperative for you to know the meanings of the energy locks. However, since not only the organ flows but also the energy locks tell us individual stories, stories about ourselves, I have decided to include the information on the meanings of the energy locks in table III (pages 42–43) for you to look into. My suggestion is to check the meaning of the energy locks you touch—and thus *open*—and meditate upon them while you activate the flow.

This mental aspect of activating your energies should not be looked down upon.

This of course applies also and specifically to your organ flows. Visualizing your organ in the color of its Depth and communicating with it, sending love and appreciation into its cells greatly enhances the manual activation by placing your hands on the appropriate energy locks.

You can try out the difference: Place your hands on the energy locks and think of some trivial thing. Then direct your thoughts into your organ, imagine it in the color of its Depth, and communicate with it by telling it how grateful you are of its precious work and how much you love it.

The difference will be immediate. Many people feel an immediate surge of energy in the respective organ, a tingling sensation or warmth . . . sometimes it actually feels like a light is being switched on inside the organ, as if the organ is the light itself (which in fact it is. Our organs ARE our lights, our tools of light to create our reality.).

However: As you may have noticed, our two 6th Depth organs (diaphragm function energy and umbilicus function energy) are not actually "physical organs," as heart or kidney energy are for example. This may make it more challenging to "imagine" them, so my advice is to simply imagine the color (light red—color of the 6th Depth for the diaphragm function energy and orange for the umbilicus function energy[1]).

So, to activate the energy flow with your hands, simply place them on the energy locks according to the instruction and as shown in the photographs. Take special care in checking your hands for right and left position and left or right hand. This also and especially applies if you want to activate the energy flow for someone else, which is a wonderful experience for both the "giver" as well as the "receiver." Make sure that you are sitting on the correct side (as shown in green letters under the activation sequence) of the person you are working on.

The self-help activation sequences can all be applied on another person as well—with one exception: the diaphragm function energy. Here we have a slightly different combination for the other person, shown below in the instruction as well as on the photograph.

# How to Activate The Diaphragm Energy Yourself

**Left side:**

Place the fingers of your left hand on the right energy lock number 14 and the fingers of your right hand on the left energy lock number 19 as shown in the photograph. Keep this position for at least 5 minutes[1] or until you feel the energy pulsing under your fingers and flowing in your body.

Left Activation
Diaphragm Energy

**Right side:** Simply reverse the sequence (to treat another person, sit on their left side):

Place the fingers of your right hand on your left energy lock number 14 and the fingers of your left hand on your right energy lock number 19 as shown in the photograph, and again keep this position for at least 5 minutes or until you feel the energy pulsing under your fingers and beginning to flow in your body.

Right Activation
Diaphragm Energy

**How to activate the diaphragm energy on someone else:**

When you activate a flow on someone else it is important that both the receiver as well as the person giving the flow are comfortable. Ideally, the receiver lies comfortably on a massage table while the person giving the flow sits on a chair on the right or left side of the receiver (according to instructions). When you activate the flow for someone else, and generally, when you place your hands on someone else's energy locks, you are the channel for the universal energy. You are actually not giving your "own" energy (even though there is in fact no such thing as your "own" energy, since ALL energy is ALWAYS universal) but rather the conductor for the infinite pool of energy of the universe. This is the reason why giving a flow for someone else will always also supply YOU with vital life energy so that both of you will profit from the energy healing session.

So, to activate the **left diaphragm flow of another person, sit on the receiver's right side (as shown in the photograph):**

Place your left hand on the receiver's left energy lock number 14 (below the left rib cage) and the right hand of the right energy lock number 19 (in the right elbow). Hold this position for five to ten minutes or until you and/or the receiver feel the energy "opening up" and starting to flow.

Left Activation of Diaphragm Flow on Someone Else

To activate the receiver's **right diaphragm flow**, sit on the **receiver's left side**:

Place your right hand on the receiver's right energy lock number 14 and your left hand on the receiver's left energy lock number 19. Again, keep this position for at least five to ten minutes or until you and/or the receiver feel the energy starting to flow harmoniously.

# The Opposition of Sagittarius Function Energy and How They Cooperate

**Sagittarius'** opposing force is the **Gemini** Soul force, which expresses itself through the stomach function energy. This means that the **stomach function energy** is the opposition flow, which supports the diaphragm energy. Activating your stomach energy acts like an extra energy infusion for you when the Moon opens the Sagittarius gate. Activating one or both sides of the stomach function while the Moon opens the Sagittarius gate will support the positive aspects of both organ functions and increase their cooperation, which in turn helps them individually.

The theme of both organ flows is **mobility** and **movement**, both physically and mentally. Furthermore, both the diaphragm as well as the stomach function energy are connected to the **lungs** and the **breathing**.

How?

Well, the diaphragm function energy for the simple reason that the diaphragm is the most important breathing muscle in the body and the stomach function energy due to the location of its Gemini Soul gate at the 2nd thoracic vertebrae, which is where energy lock number 3 is located. Energy lock number 3 is also known as the **gateway to the lungs,** which shows us why the stomach energy is a key factor in the activation of the lung function.

In order to support the oppositional cooperation of these two organ flows, or if you feel you need an extra energy boost during Sagittarius days, simply add the activation sequence of the Stomach function energy (which you can find in the appropriate chapter) to your activation program during Sagittarius days.

# General Tips and Facts for
# Sagittarius Days

**Massaging the Soul Gate:**

Besides opening your current Soul gate energetically, you may also make contact with it on the physical level by gently massaging it for one to two minutes first thing in the morning. Doing this is a great way to become conscious of the gates of your Soul on your personal zodiac, which is YOU!

To massage your Soul gate, dip your fingers into some extra virgin oil (for example almond or olive oil) and then massage the Sagittarius Soul gate at the umbilicus by gently moving the fingers clockwise.

While doing this you may imagine your Sagittarius Soul gate as well as the area around the umbilicus, in purple red, the color of Sagittarius, or of course, in bright red, the color of 6th Depth.

## Music / musical key:

Listening to music in the current musical key activated by the moon is a great way to further enhance the positive effects of tuning into the cosmic symphony of creation.

My suggestion: Listen to a piece of music in F Major while activating the diaphragm function energy, and experience the vibration activated by the moon with all your senses in the very sense of the word!

The daily musical key given to us by the moon is the reason why music is perceived differently on different days by the audience. A musical piece in F Major played on a Sagittarius day has a much stronger and heartfelt effect on the Soul level than if it is played on another day of the Moon's journey through the zodiac.

This is a fact well worthwhile to try out for yourself.

If you are a musician or music manager, it is well worth getting into the habit of planning concerts according to the moon's position, which for example means: On a day when the cosmic symphony due to the moon's position in the gate of Sagittarius sounds in F Major, the perfect musical key to choose for your concert would be F Major!

Try it out and hear and FEEL the difference!

**Physical exercise:**

Since the diaphragm function energy is an **ascending flow**, flowing upwards from the chest, any physical exercise involving stretching the chest muscle, like **rowing** or **breaststroke** swimming, as well as certain Yoga exercises, would be an ideal choice during Sagittarius days. And—since the Sagittarius vibration is such an outgoing energy with an inviting effect for people to get together, Sagittarius days are **perfect days for social events and for making new friends.**

**Last but not least:**

Sagittarius represents the merging of the primordial fire of the 6th Depth with the fire of Sagittarius. Thus we have the double Fire element reigning during Sagittarius days, a time of fiery energy inviting you to get out and speak the[[something missing here]] and for the TRUTH. This is why Sagittarius days are great for all that has to do with **Truth, Justice,** and **Love.**

Take advantage of this vibration by arranging dates when the emphasis is on Truth and Justice.

**Sagittarius days are the perfect days to get married.**

**And—one last suggestion follows on the next page.**

# Become **CONSCIOUS** of the **Moon's**
## vibration around you!

Since the Moon's vibration is particularly obvious during early morning and late evening hours, you should make it a habit to watch the sun rise and set while being mentally aware of the current vibration activated by the moon. Why not use the early morning hours for an energizing moon meditation, envisaging Sagittarius' energy enlighten your body.

Discover for yourself how the current moon vibration shows in the colors of the sky, which during Sagittarius days is generally illuminated in the most stunning red and purple colors, whereas on other days the colors may be much softer or even have a bright red glow, like during Scorpio days.

Discovering the daily vibration through nature (as well as obviously through yourself by activating the flows and feeling their energy) is getting to know YOURSELF. Since in the universe there is no such thing as "division" . . . in the end we are all ONE—YOU are the energy that forms and creates the world—and so is your neighbor, your child, your partner . . . we are infinite energy merging the 12 different aspects of the ONE energy into our reality—continuously and eternally—until we have become CONSCIOUS of our infinite potential, making room for a new planet and a new realm of existence.

UMBILICUS GATE /
SEXUAL ORGANS /
PUBIC BONE

# THE MOON OPENS THE COSMIC GATE OF
# CAPRICORN

*You Open Your Capricorn Soul Gate through the*
*Vibration of Umbilicus Function Energy*

### Capricorn says:
### "I MANIFEST the LIGHT in my LIFE!

From Sagittarius gate the moon continues its endless circle around the Earth into the gate of Capricorn. We are still in 6th Depth, the level of "mediation" between heaven and Earth, the kingdom of the **Moon.** By entering the gate of Capricorn however, the moon invites you to enter the realm of physical, Earthly pleasure . . . Your Soul Gate of Capricorn is located at your pubic bone, the root chakra . . . it is here that **reproduction** and **fertility**, yes indeed CREATION of new life, has its beginning. Capricorn may and IS often seen as a rather "cool" star sign and energy. When we take the location of the Soul Gate as well as the element of the mother Depth, the 6th Depth, the primordial fire, into account, it becomes clear that the vibration of Capricorn has in fact a totally different side to it—a nurturing, creative, warm, and mediating side.

**G Major** is the musical key attributed to Capricorn and its key organ energy umbilicus function—it activates the creative expression and refines both the mental and emotional aspects of your being. If you could *see* the vibration of Capricorn with your physical eyes you would see the bright orange color of the Hindu Sannyasins, the Vedic monks in their renunciation stage. Interestingly, orange is also the color of the sacral chakra, the second chakra connected to feelings, emotions, pleasure, sensuality, intimacy, and connection, as well as of the whole area known as the Hara, the area between the umbilicus and the pubic bone.

It is an energy center of extreme importance to your overall wellbeing and your ability to overcome negativity.

I always like to remind myself of what a well-known Indian Ayurvedic doctor told me about the area of the Hara and the color ORANGE: He said that whenever a negative thought crosses your mind or a negative experience makes you feel sad, you should immediately concentrate on the color ORANGE and on your Hara between the umbilicus and pubic bone . . . you should in fact go right into this area and color with your thoughts and totally merge with the color orange. You should BECOME the color orange yourself and this will then TRANSFORM any negativity into positive energy.

And most interestingly, this Ayurvedic doctor also told me that the color orange and the whole area of the Hara and of the sexual organs corresponds—how else should and could it be?—to the MOON!

Remember that the Moon governs 6th Depths, the mother-Depth of Capricorn and its key organ flow umbilicus function energy.

So, what is the umbilicus function energy? It is one of the most important energies of your body. Just like the other 6th Depth organ function, the diaphragm energy, it is not a physical organ. 6th Depth has a higher, finer vibration than physical existence; it is the all-encompassing Depth BEFORE physical existence; it is the *developing* of physical existence.

And this is precisely the reason why activating your **umbilicus energy** is so highly beneficial to your wellbeing! ALL physical problems originate in the energy body; they originate in the energy we use to CREATE our physical body as well as our reality (which is also the reason why the body and our reality are intrinsically linked together).

Activating and lovingly nurturing this "pre-physical" energy gives you the ability to create the base for a strong, vibrant body and for the formation of the reality you desire.

Umbilicus function energy is a **descending** flow, taking on the energy of its predecessor diaphragm energy at the lateral side of the ring fingernail (see also graphic showing flowpath of the umbilicus function energy (pages 70–71). The energy descends[9] down the back of the arm and shoulders to the third rib between the breasts. Part of the flow then continues into the heart, another branch flows into gallbladder and stomach, and yet another flows to the backside of the ear diagonally through the head, reemerges at the medial side of the eyebrow, and flows to the lateral part of the eye.

The flowpath gives us a hint about umbilicus functions' ability to ease headaches and ear problems, but because of the high vibration of 6th Depth, this flow should not be looked at only from the flowpath point of view.

In Far East Asian philosophy and medicine, umbilicus function energy is known as triple warmer energy—and this is self-explanatory, meaning, umbilicus function energy brings warmth and harmony to body, mind, and Soul and harmonizes the trinity of **breast** (breathing), **waist** (digestion), and **hips** (elimination).

Umbilicus function energy opens the heart—for the beautiful things in life as well as for abundance—ABUNDANCE, which is there ALL the time, which YOU yourself are! Except you often do not realize it—because your fine heart energy may be blocked—and umbilicus function energy helps precisely here: It has a very spiritual effect on your heart—it "warms" the heart and thus YOU through your heart, the seat of Spirit! In the life-frame of Man, umbilicus time is associated with the time of conception through the whole pregnancy until (and including) the age of 3. (See table II.)

During this time life is ruled by umbilicus function energy, which also means that any trauma happening at this time of life will affect umbilicus function energy and leave an energetical scar, which—if left un"treated"—may in later life cause problems in any of the succeeding organ flows.

To understand this, we need to imagine our twelve organ flows as ONE big flow—which they, in their totality, are! One big flow made up of 12 "individual" organ flows flowing into each other—energizing and nurturing each other—OR—if there are problems in one flow—handing them on to the succeeding flow and the following flows!

There is no such thing as a "most important flow." Each of the 12 organ flows is of vital importance in its own right; however, since umbilicus function is the "first" flow in a person's life (since it rules conception as well as pregnancy) it is often regarded as a "base" flow.

If umbilicus function energy is out of harmony, all the other flows will automatically suffer—and be undernourished.

So, nourish your umbilicus function energy and you will nourish and vitalize your life!

Whenever the moon resides in the cosmic gate of Capricorn, activate your umbilicus function energy by applying the following simple energy lock combination:

# Flowpath of Umbilicus Energy

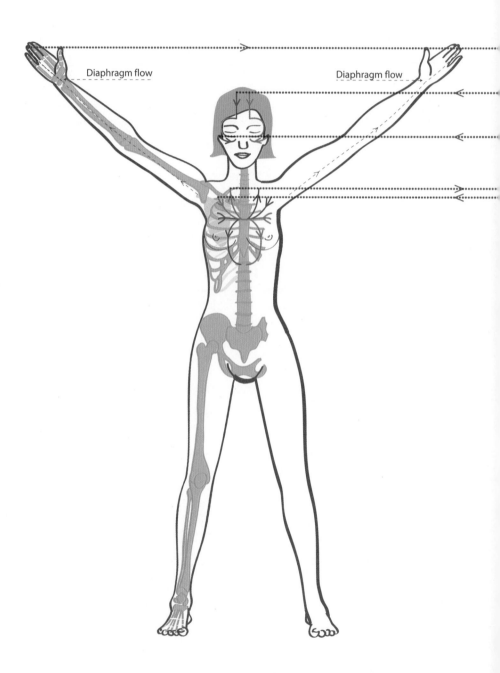

Diaphragm flow

Diaphragm flow

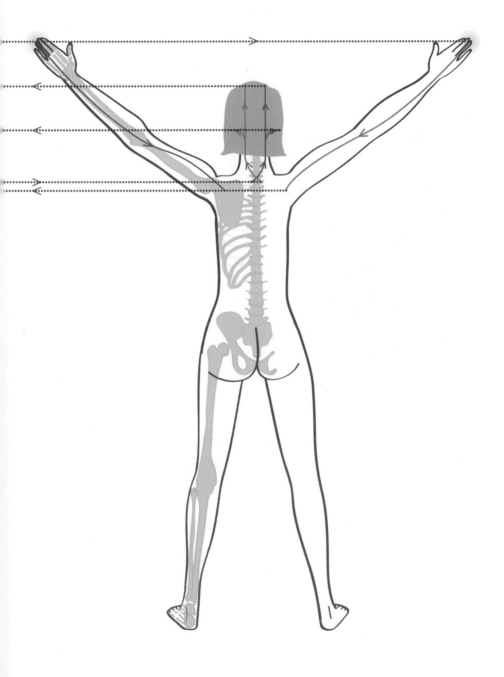

# Activating the Capricorn Energy Flow
# Umbilicus Function Energy

Right Activation Umbilicus
Function Energy

**Left side:** (to treat another person sit on her left side)

Place the fingers of your left hand on the right energy lock number 20 and the fingers of your right hand on the left energy lock number 19. Keep this position for at least 5 minutes[1] or until you feel the energy pulsing under your fingers and flowing in your body.

**Right side:** Simply reverse the sequence (to treat another person sit on her right side).

Place the fingers of your right hand on your left energy lock number 20 and the fingers of your left hand on your right energy lock number 19 as shown in the photograph, and again keep this position for at least 5 minutes or until you feel the energy pulsing under your fingers and beginning to flow in your body.

## The Opposition of Umbilicus Function Energy and How They Cooperate

The opposition flow of umbilicus function energy is the spleen energy of cancer. Umbilicus and spleen function energy—along with kidney function energy—can be seen as the most important organ functions for anything to do with fertility, pregnancy, sexuality, as well as generally "feeling comfortable within your body."

Just as umbilicus function energy welcomes you in your body, so does spleen function energy make you feel "at home."

Spleen function is the nurturing, motherly energy of your body. It is "the moon" within your microcosmos, while umbilicus corresponds to the vibration of the Earth.

Umbilicus vibrates in G Major, the musical key of our planet Earth, of your DNA, the vibration of mediation and manifestation, whereas spleen energy vibrates half a tone up, that is G-sharp Major, which corresponds to the vibration of the moon.

Activating umbilicus function energy and spleen function energy after each other lets you BE ONE with the dance of creation of moon and Earth . . . the endless creation of reality out of Rhea, the eternal Life Flow.

Furthermore, umbilicus and spleen function in harmony are essential for anything to do with the immune system. **Autoimmune disorders** are a sign of your Soul— or let's rather say—a cry for help from umbilicus and spleen function energy and their harmonious cooperation.

If you suffer from autoimmune disorders such as, for example, MS, caring for your umbilicus and spleen function energy is absolutely essential.

"Caring" for these energies means activating them when the moon gives you their vibration by passing the corresponding cosmic gates of Capricorn and Cancer—as well as looking after these energies in between.

Spleen energy is the one body function energy that I would suggest you do each day (alternating between the right and left side) as a "base energy" for your system.

I personally activate one side of my spleen energy each day on top of the daily moon flow. It gets me centered and supplies me with great Earthly strength, since spleen function energy—as we will learn in the spleen chapter—is an ascending flow that starts the toes, thus bringing the energy of Earth into your whole body— like a flower distributing the energy it receives from Earth via its roots to the leaves and flower blossom.

To enhance the cooperation of umbilicus and spleen function energy simply add the activation sequence of spleen function energy to your activation program when the moon is opening the gate of Capricorn.

# General Tips and Facts for
# Capricorn Days

**Massaging the Soul Gate:**

Your Capricorn Soul Gate is located at the pubic bone and should be gently massaged on Capricorn days.

To do this, simply dip your fingers into some extra virgin oil (for example, almond or olive oil) and then massage the Capricorn Soul Gate at the pubic bone by gently moving the fingers clockwise.

While doing this, imagine your Capricorn Soul Gate, as well as the area around the pubic bone, in dark blue, the color of Capricorn, or of course in bright red, the color of 6th Depth, or in bright orange, which, as you have learned, is the color corresponding to G as in G Major, the musical key of Capricorn; see below.

**Music / musical key:**

**G Major** is Capricorn's musical key—and what a beautiful and harmonious key this is.

G Major has an invigorating, yet at the same time, calming and relaxing effect. Just as umbilicus function energy releases headaches, so do musical pieces in G Major help against headache.

G is the tone, the vibration of the Earth. The more harmonious your umbilicus function energy vibrates, the more you are IN TUNE with our planet Earth, your home during incarnation. Being "in tune" with the tone G means your DNA vibrates in perfect union with EARTH.

**Physical exercise:**

Anything that brings you in contact with Earth, like walking or hiking, is perfect on Capricorn days! Get outside, FEEL the Earth under your feet, embrace a tree, lie on the hot sand, and/or do yoga on the beach or on a meadow.

Yoga comes from the sanscrit word "yuga" for connection—the connection of heaven and Earth, of Spirit and body, the connection that YOU yourself ARE through umbilicus function energy!

**Last but not least:**

Umbilicus represents the merging of the primordial fire of the 6th Depth with the Earth of Capricorn.

Capricorn days are perfect days for **manifesting** your dreams! GO FOR IT! And get things done!

Capricorn follows Sagittarius, which—as you know—is the spark coming into manifestation. Sagittarius is not a real step in creation yet. It is the ending and the beginning—the idea.

With Capricorn, however, this idea starts to manifest. We "take it into our hands"— and this is not only symbolical but should be understood in the truest sense of the word, since umbilicus function energy of Capricorn—as you can see from the graphic showing the flowpath, pages 70–71, takes over the energy of its predecessor diaphragm energy in the hands . . . to be precise at the outer ring fingernail, then taking the energy into the face . . . into the obvious!
Thus Capricorn days are perfect days for important contract negotiations and presentations. Buying a house or founding a new company (for example) will have all the positive energy of the universe behind.

Take Life into your own Hands—make it yours—USE Capricorns Earthly energy by activating it's flow and/or holding the palm of your hands (general harmonizer for 6th Depths) as often and as long as possible.

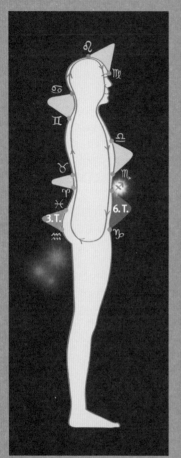

# 3rd Depth—Green Point-of-Star
## QUINTESSENCE

The MOON travels through the 3rd Depth
and opens the Cosmic Gate of AQUARIUS followed
by the Cosmic Gate of PISCES.

For you this means that you reach SOURCE
by opening your . . .

AQUARIUS Soul Gate *through* the vibration
of GALLBLADDER Function Energy,

followed by your . . .

PISCES Soul Gate *through* the vibration
of LIVER Function Energy!

# The Quintessence of 3rd Depth
## The KEY

**The green point-of-star is the "head"
of your five-pointed star. It is the KEY to unfolding
the remaining four star points.**

The first point-of-star, which you unfold, is the head of your five-pointed star, governed by the planet Jupiter, also known as the planet of expansion and luck.

3rd Depth is ALL about **expansion** and about being **creative**. Whenever the moon enters the green area on the zodiac, the cosmic gates of Aquarius and Pisces, the cosmic vibration urges you to get your creative juices flowing . . . to allow new ideas to blossom and to BE the cosmic flow of new creation yourself.

Strictly speaking, creation begins in 3rd Depth—the green point-of-star. 7th Depth is UNITY, the level of the Sun. In order to KNOW itself, unity needs to divide itself . . . needs to "unfold" into diversion . . . into positive and negative, black and white, male and female.

6th Depth is the mediator between UNITY and DIVERSION. As such, it is both unity and diversion (strictly speaking, so are all the other Depths as well, since they are all part of the cosmic egg, which IS 6th Depth).

With 3rd Depth, now we cross the bridge into "manifestation," and this is why 3rd Depth is in effect also known as "the bridge."

The bridge between heaven and Earth, or—to put it in "our human terms"—the bridge between your ideas and their manifestation.

Opening your Aquarius Soul Gate by activating gallbladder function energy as well as your Pisces Soul Gate by activating your liver energy for you means crossing the bridge between heaven and Earth—and—more importantly—keeping it OPEN during the whole process of manifestation.

The idea, the spark of the eternal flame, has its home in 7th Depth, and despite the fact that the spark decides to experience itself as "individual," it ALWAYS remains ONE with SOURCE—through 3rd Depth—which is exactly why opening and keeping your 3rd Depth gates, Aquarius Soul Gate and Pisces Soul Gate open is ESSENTIAL, not only for health and wellbeing but also for the realization of your dreams.

3rd Depth in harmony gives you **flexibility**—both mental as well as physical. It enables you to SEE physically but also on a spiritual level and to **distinguish.** The ability to distinguish—as you will see in the 5th Depth chapter—also relates to Virgo, which is the opposition force of Pisces. Pisces and Virgo in harmony "open" your spiritual and physical eyes, in the truest sense of its word.

3rd Depth can be your **key to success**—but, if in dis-harmony, it can also be your spiral into severe chronic dis-ease(s) such as cancer or utter despair and destruction and negative emotions such as **hate** and **jealousy.**

3rd Depth, and thus gallbladder energy and/or livery energy in disharmony can and will destroy the body. It will let you feel and look "burned-out" and prematurely aged, with wrinkly skin, weak eyes, and an emaciated body.

The great news, however, is that—despite your physical condition, despite your weakness and visible age of your body—harmonizing 3rd Depth can and WILL always enable you to stand up again and regenerate, yes, **REJUVENATE**, completely.

In this respect, it reminds me of the quality of the Major Arcana card XX Judgment from the *Rider-Waite Tarot*. This beautiful Major Arcana shows people rising from tombs of the dead to an angel playing the trumpet in the sky.

The only limits there are, are the ones in your head!

The green point of the star with its cosmic gates of Aquarius and Pisces can and WILL enable you to rise after defeat and chronic illness. It is your key to fulfil your life's potential and to unfold the other four points of the Star which you yourself ARE.

# Harmonizing the 3rd Depth
## Middle Finger

The "quickie method" of harmonizing 3rd Depth, your KEY, is the middle finger. Whenever the moon passes the green area on the zodiac, your middle finger is the finger that will harmonize your whole being by connecting you to Source.

Holding your middle finger harmonizes your 3rd Depth organs as well as a multitude of body functions (remember, that each finger harmonizes 14,400 body functions). AND—with the middle finger being the obvious "center" of your hand, or rather, the extension of the center of your hand—holding your middle finger acts like a general harmonizer, thus harmonizing not only 3rd Depths Quintessence but also all the other Depths and elements of your body.

Wrap the fingers of your left hand around the middle finger of your right hand and keep this position for a few minutes. (Ideally for twenty minutes, but even holding it for only three minutes already has a positive effect on your body functions and emotion).

Then change hands and wrap the fingers of your right hand around your left middle finger. Again keep this position for at least three to five minutes, ideally for twenty minutes.

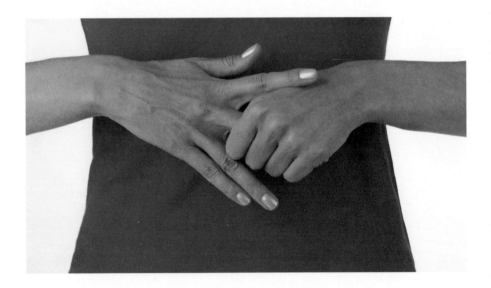

# General Tips for the Moon's Journey through the 3rd Depth

- 3rd Depth is all about **seeing** and the **eyes**. Thus, when the moon travels through 3rd Depth, reading late at night and with dim light is especially harmful to your eyes and in fact to your whole wellbeing. **Green** is the color of 3rd Depth and this means that gazing into the lush green of a spring forest, for example, has an extremely regenerating effect not only on your eyes but generally.

- And: Why not daydream a little? Daydreaming can transport you into beautiful zones. You choose which and at the same time be assured that your body regenerates in a very effective way.

Unlike what many teachers tell schoolchildren, daydreaming is NOT harmful but necessary. It is a natural regenerative process that enables you to reconnect with Source whenever and wherever you are. And—why not at the same time hold your middle finger—3rd Depths harmonizing finger and thus making your dream journey even more powerful and effective? Let your mind drift off . . . and come back totally regenerated.

- **Food/taste:** With green being the color of 3rd Depth, anything fresh and green will help your 3rd Depth and thus your blood. 3rd Depth is related to **blood essence**, the vibration of blood. And since green is the color of Chlorophyll, anything, the blood of the plants, any fresh green leaves are an amazing 3rd Depth and vitality enhancer. Why not start your day with a green power smoothie—ideally together with lemon juice, which can be seen both as sour and bitter. **Sour** is the taste of 3rd Depth, which means that sour foods, such as vinegar, for example, will help 3rd Depth and activate both liver and gallbladder.

*Sour makes you happy* is a German proverb, which again shows that the knowledge about the Depths and cosmic forces is deeply rooted in human.

Include some sour foods in your diet each day and of course especially when the moon is traveling through the green gates, the cosmic gates of Aquarius and Pisces, and feel the difference this small but important addition to your diet makes.

A great and extremely healthy way to start your day is to squeeze the juice of one (or more) lemon(s) into a glass and fill it with lukewarm water. You may add a bit of ginger powder to it or just drink it pure. Then wait for about half an hour until breakfast, and let the juice do its cleansing work.

This simple but extremely healthy recipe alkalizes and cleanses your blood. An alkaline level of blood is essential to remain healthy and to heal. If you keep your blood on an alkaline level, dis-eases such as cancer or other chronic "projects" will not manifest. Dis-ease depends on the condition of your blood—and the condition of your blood depends on the harmony of your 3rd Depth.

# 3rd Depth and Emotional Growth

Anger and hate are sure signs of 3rd Depth in distress. They are in fact signs of the Soul disconnecting or being disconnected from the body. A disconnected Soul is always the beginning of dis-ease. Some people actually dream and feel this "dis-connection" very vividly. It is a feeling of "being lost," being dis-tached from your Source, your true home.

Harmonizing 3rd Depth is attaching your Soul to your True Self again. It is "coming home" to what you really ARE—what you were born to BE.

Activating and harmonizing 3rd Depth transforms negative emotions such as anger and hate into . . .


**CREATIVITY, PATIENCE, and GENEROSITY!**

# Wind and Thunderstorms!

3rd Depth is all about breaking barriers and unfolding your potential. Contrary to the gentle, but equally strong 4th Depth energy of water (which we will talk about in the 4th Depth chapter), 3rd Depth has the urge to "break free" and remove obstacles—no matter what. It is the energy of beginning—it is the first point-of-star unfolding itself—leading the way for the unfolding of the remaining 4 points of star. In nature this energy shows up as "strong winds," thunderstorms, and even earthquakes. When the moon enters the green part of the Zodiac, the 3rd Depth gates nearly always will respond with wind. See and feel it for yourself; watch nature, be part of it, because you ARE nature itself. The same principle thus applies to you—and humans in general. 3rd Depth days are the time when "discussions" can turn out nasty, when anger that may have been stored for far too long in your liver and gallbladder rises up, and lets you and/or others explode. 3rd Depth carries the strongest and wildest energy of all Depth. USE this energy instead of letting it destroy you. 3rd Depth in dis-harmony, anger, hate, and jealousy, can destroy the body completely—just as a hurricane leaves utter destruction. **Cancer** and **burnout-Syndrome** are symptoms of a 3rd Depth imbalance—an imbalance that will show as anger and frustration before moving on onto your body.

Listen to the voice of your Soul—do not let 3rd Depth destroy you, but consciously choose to USE its amazing creative energy—by activating its organ forces gallbladder and liver and/or by simply holding your middle finger—your KEY to total harmony whenever the moon travels through the gates of Aquarius and Pisces.

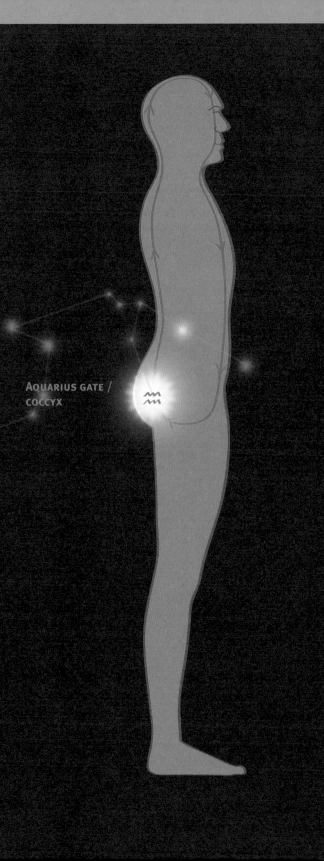

AQUARIUS GATE /
COCCYX

# THE MOON OPENS THE COSMIC GATE OF
# AQUARIUS

*You Open Your Aquarius Soul Gate through the*
*Vibration of Gallbladder Function Energy*

**Aquarius** says:
**"I KNOW** that I am a child of Heaven!"

When the moon enters the cosmic gate of Aquarius, the whole universe vibrates in the beautifully cheerful musical key A Major. A Major was the favorite musical key of Wolfgang Amadeus Mozart—who was himself born under the sign of Aquarius. Mozart was the perfect representation of Aquarius energy—cheerful, incredibly creative, workaholic, with an amazing strive for perfection and knowledge.

This IS Aquarius energy at its best. This is how YOU want Aquarius to function through your **Gallbladder energy**.

Have a look at the illustration of the gallbladder flow, and see how gallbladder energy flows through your body. Gallbladder energy takes over from its predecessor Umbilicus function energy below the eyes, where the yellow flash can be seen. One branch flows in circular movements at the sides of the head over the head; the other one continues its flowpath down the front of the body, with one branch scattering in the stomach and the other way circling to the back of the body, around the hip (which explains why gallbladder energy is THE number one hip flow and can—will, if cared for properly—prevent hip problems or even hip replacements) and down along the sides of the legs, into the 4th toe and the big toe—where it will then transform into the Liver energy.

Gallbladder in disharmony thus shows in many ways other than discomfort in your gallbladder. Severe headaches and migraines are usually linked to this strong and fierce energy, which, in its "worst" disharmonic form, can and will destroy the body and disconnect the Soul from its source.

Complaints linked to gallbladder energy may show anywhere along its flowpath: The head, the eyes (nervous twitching under the eyes is usually a sign of either Umbilicus function or Gallbladder energy in disharmony), Umbilicus, since it is the predecessor, which transforms into Gallbladder energy under the eyes. The point under the eyes is, so to speak, the "switch" point between the two energies. And—as is the case with any "change," switch, and transformation—there can or may be problems during this change. Practically speaking this means that when you experience nervous twitching under your eyes, it is advisable to first activate your Gallbladder energy (thus clearing the way) and then also "push" from behind activating Umbilicus function energy.

This, however, should ALWAYS be done on top of the activation of the daily Moon flow—your key flow. You will, however, notice that your symptoms most of the time coincide with the moon—that is—people who usually do not suffer from nervous twitching under the eye, will suddenly start to experience it when the moon is either traveling through the gates of Capricorn or Aquarius—OR through their opposition gates Cancer or Leo. In fact, symptoms of specific organ flows OFTEN do appear when the moon prevails in its opposition gate. This is due to the fact that at that point the energy in opposition to the moon's location is at its weakest point—thus showing and "speaking up" through symptoms.

It is my strong advice, however, to always stick to your current moon flow and add the opposition flow on top of it. Do not leave the moon flow aside simply because you may experience other symptoms. The moon flow is ALWAYS your key flow, linking you directly to SOURCE, and thus supplying ALL other energies and organs with the vital energy of LIFE—directly from 7th Depth, the golden light of TRUTH.

Aquarius gate is located at the coccyx, which means that by activating your gallbladder flow you energetically unblock and open your coccyx. Unblocking your coccyx is vital for the energy to be able to freely flow up the spine. If your energy gets stuck at or around your coccyx, it will not be able to reach your brain and supply it with vital life energy. A brain without energy is something I do not need to go into here. Anybody knows that in order for the brain to be able to "think" and "function," it needs vital energy and oxygen—otherwise, it will shut off.

I once knew a lady who suffered from dizziness for years. Due to this condition she had to give up working, her relationship failed, and she lost all faith in life. Standing and/or walking was nearly impossible for her—the only thing she could basically do was sit in a chair or lie in bed. Then she took part in a Jin Shin class where she received a 3rd Depth flow opening her coccyx. After all these years a blockage that had been caused by a long-forgotten heavy fall on the bottom, finally opened and enabled the energy to finally flow up again to the brain. After years of "trying out everything," the woman finally regained her life—thanks to this simple but incredibly efficient key of activating 3rd Depth and opening gallbladder energy.

To sum it up, Gallbladder energy—together with Bladder function energy, another descending flow—is the number one anti-headache flow. Besides activating the Gallbladder function, it also helps the Liver energy as well as all digestive organs. Gallbladder energy in balance will help to make decisions and help against indecisiveness. Gallbladder energy is also the flow that will let you finish projects. Aquarius individuals are sometimes known for starting many things and not finishing them. Gallbladder energy keeps your hips supple and gives your whole body flexibility.

It fills you with vibrant creativity and enables you to create masterpieces in whatever field you may choose to do so.

# Flowpath of Gallbladder Energy

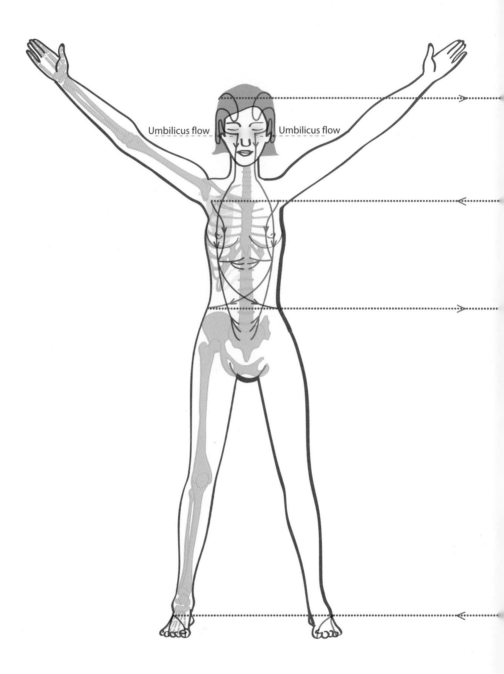

Umbilicus flow    Umbilicus flow

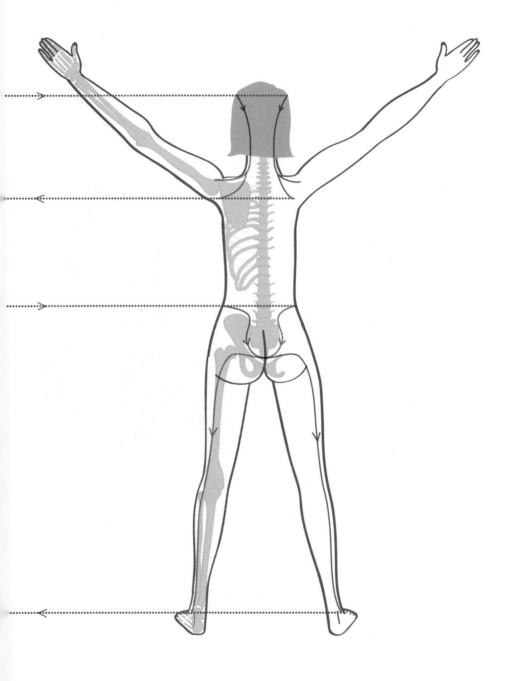

# Activating the Aquarius Energy Flow
## Gallbladder Function Energy

**Left side:** (To treat another person sit on her right side)

Place the fingers of your left hand on your left energy lock number 12 and the fingers of your right hand on your right energy lock number 20. Keep this position for at least five minutes[1] or until you feel the energy pulsing under your fingers and flowing in your body.

**Right side:** Simply reverse the sequence (to treat another person sit on her left side).

Place the fingers of your right hand on your right energy lock number 12 and the fingers of your left hand on your left energy lock number 20. Keep this position for at least five minutes or until you feel the energy pulsing under your fingers and beginning to flow in your body.

Left Activation
Gallbladder Energy

# The Opposition of Gallbladder Function Energy and How They Cooperate

The opposition flow of gallbladder function energy is your heart energy. Heart is the key energy of Leo—and Leo is the opposition sign of Aquarius.

How do gallbladder and its energy cooperate, and what do they have in common?

Let's first have a look at the position of the two Soul Gates. Aquarius Soul Gate as you know lies at your coccyx and thus at the beginning of the ascending flow of the Life Flow.

Leo Soul Gate on the other hand lies right at the other end on the top of your head—on your crown chakra—in fact, it IS your crown chakra.

The crown chakra is the highest energy center of man. It is your spiritual gate to your Higher Self—vibrating in the most beautiful golden and purple colors when it is open.

Opening your Leo Soul Gate does not solely depend on the harmony of your heart energy—the key energy for Leo. It also depends on Aquarius energy. If your Aquarius Soul Gate is closed, the energy will not even get up the spine. It will stay at the bottom of your spine and may even flow "backward" towards your pubic bone, your sexual and digestive organs, and cause considerable discomfort there.
Opening Aquarius Soul Gate, therefore, is essential for all the following Soul Gates along the spine—and especially for your Leo Soul Gate. If, however, Leo Soul Gate is closed, it will send the energy streaming up the spine right backwards down the spine —which is just as bad as a closed Aquarius Soul Gate.

So, does it make sense to you that you should always strive to open BOTH opposition Soul Gates? It is not a bad idea to open the opposition Soul Gate (in this case Leo on top of the head) BEFORE the actual Moon-gate in order to "make room" for the energy to flow up (or down depending on which Soul Gates you are working with).

Anger, by the way, is one of the most harmful emotions for the heart. And as you know, anger is the emotion that occurs when 3rd Depth is in disharmony. Harmonizing 3rd Depth will ALWAYS help your heart. The middle finger, the harmonizing finger of 3rd Depth, opens energy lock 13—the main energy lock for the heart chakra, located on your chest in the area of your 3rd vertebrae. Energy lock number 13 enables Self LOVE and loving your SELF is the key to loving AND to being loved.

And . . . there is another thing worth mentioning in the cooperation of Aquarius and Leo energy. Can you guess what it is?

Imagine Aquarius Soul Gate at the bottom of your spine and Leo Soul Gate at the top of your spine.

Thinking of these two gates . . . what comes to your mind?
I am sure you guessed it. It is the Life Flow and the spine being the physical aspect of the Life Flow itself.

Activating your gallbladder energy as well as its opposition force heart energy and thus opening their respective gates will activate the ascending flow of the Life Flow and straighten and strengthen your spine thus enabling you to regain your PRIDE— very fitting for Leo energy.

# General Tips and Facts for Aquarius Days

**Massaging the Soul Gate:**

Your Aquarius Soul Gate is located at the **coccyx** and should be gently massaged on Aquarius days.

To do this, simply dip your fingers into some extra virgin oil (for example, almond or olive oil), and then massage your Soul Gate at the coccyx by gently moving the fingers clockwise.

While doing this, imagine your **Aquarius Soul Gate**, as well as the area around the pubic bone, in blue-violet, the color of Aquarius, and imagine the energy rise up your spine from your Aquarius Soul Gate.

**Music/musical key:**

**A Major** is Aquarius musical key—and when I think of A Major, I think of W. A. Mozart. As I mentioned already, W. A. Mozart was born under the sign of Aquarius and he loved A Major's cheerful and bright energy. A Major is like Mozart the man was himself: full of cheerfulness and cheekiness, ready to party and have a great time. A Major is the vibration of happiness. Activate your Gallbladder energy and play your body, your instrument of your Soul, in this beautiful key.

**Physical exercise:**

3rd Depth days invite you to do gentle exercises, which increase flexibility, such as stretching, Pilates, or Qi Gong.
Anything too strenuous, such as vigorous jogging, is harmful on green moon days and should thus be avoided. Also, 3rd Depth days are the least ideal days to start a new exercise regimen.

This is much better done on either Aries or Sagittarius days.
3rd Depth days are all about gentle flexibility. Sudden and disruptive experiences that cause trauma to body and Soul can and will harm 3rd Depth more than any other Depth but can of course also be healed by using 3rd Depth flows and/or holding your middle finger.

*By caring for and activating 3rd Depth, you invite your Soul back into your body!*

**Last but not least:**

Aquarius days are a time of great intellectual stimulation. Use this knowledge for fruitful teamwork and place important appointments for creative brainstorming on days when the moon resides in Aquarius. A great way to enhance intellectually brilliant thinking and cooperation is by beginning teamwork sessions by collectively holding the middle finger for a few minutes. This "moon-trick" avoids stubbornness, conflict, or other minor or major disasters and stimulates creativity.

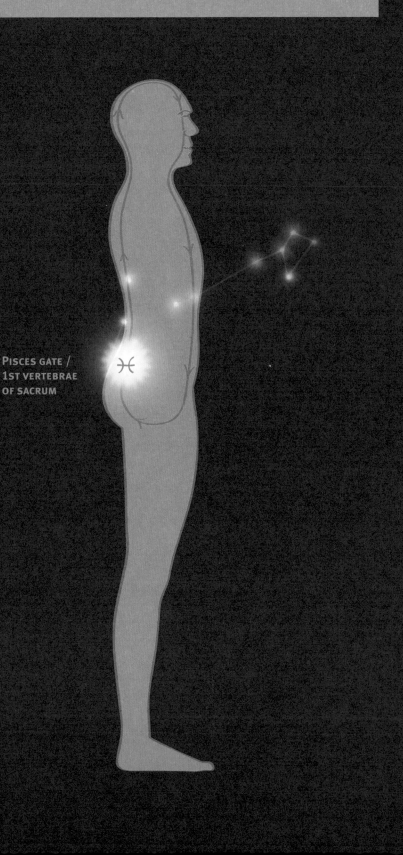

PISCES GATE /
1ST VERTEBRAE
OF SACRUM

# THE MOON OPENS THE COSMIC GATE OF
# PISCES

*You Open Your Pisces Soul Gate through the*
*Vibration of Liver Function Energy*

### Pisces say:
### "I BELIEVE in the TRUTH!

Pisces Soul Gate follows Aquarius Soul Gate, and **Liver function** energy is the key to open your Pisces Soul Gate at the first vertebrae of sacrum. S a c r u m contains in it the syllable "sacred," and is derived from the Latin word *Sacrum* = sacred object.

Legend says that the sacrum is "the part of the body that enables man to rise from death."

In German, Sacrum is called "Kreuz-Bein," which directly translated means "cross-leg."

The cross being the 4 principles of Earth, the 4 elements of the Zodiac, man's destiny, AND key to heaven, to eternal life. Within the cosmic code of creation (3 x 4 = 12), the 4 is the "obstacle"(the cross) containing in itself the spark (the 3) and thus the key to fulfill itself and become 12 = 3 . . . 3 having become CONSCIOUS of itself!

When you think of the cross, you think of Christ—and when you think of Christ, you think of Pisces, since the Age of Pisces coincided with the birth of Christ.

Christ came to Earth to take on man's suffering—to transform it and to give us the key to establish the golden Jerusalem on Earth ourselves.

And just as Christ took on man's suffering, so does the liver, the key energy to open your gate of Pisces, take on negativity not just from all the other organs but from any emotion and any thought that crosses your mind and that you expose yourself to.

The liver is the organ of "suffering" BUT has an amazing ability to transform negativity and to regenerate itself and by doing this to regenerate YOU again.

If the liver is healthy, you are healthy. Yes, it is as simple as that. It is not by chance that in Hawaii a popular greeting is, "How is your liver today?" meaning "How are YOU today?"

A strained liver makes you grumpy and overly emotional (which is maybe why Pisceans—whose key organ is the liver—are sometimes known as being overly emotional).

Liver is the number one organ to cure cancer. It is a master-laboratory that digests all your emotions, feelings, and thoughts . . . and carries them on to all the other organs and cells of your body.

Take a minute to try out the following "exercise." Place your right hand on your liver (the right hand for the simple reason that the liver is located under the right rib cage). Imagine the whole area under your right rib cage in a beautiful bright emerald green, the color of 3rd Depth, our current point-of-star. LOVE your liver— tell your liver that you LOVE it—talk to it, communicate with it, the tool of your Soul.

After a few minutes you will feel your liver respond—be it with a tingling sensation or simply a feeling of warmth in the area of your liver. This tingling or warmth is the energy of HEALING, which the liver will be happy to spread in your whole body—working for you and reacting to your life—being the mirror of your Soul, not just its tool.

If you want, then continue to try out the opposite. Keep your hand under your right rib cage, but change your thoughts to "negativity"—to some unpleasant recent experience, for example, a person for whom you feel "negative emotions"—and see and feel the difference after just a few minutes. The beautiful expansion created by your loving thoughts will change to a feeling of "tightening" and "feeling blocked." It is as if you switch a switch from right (healing/health) to left (blocking/restricting).

This exercise, by the way, can and should also be done while activating the flows . . . thinking of the respective colors of the Depths for the organ you activate, so green for liver, bright red for the heart, and yellow for spleen to name just a few.

Just like Aquarius gallbladder energy, liver energy enhances **creativity.** Pisceans thrive when being creative, and blocking this inner need may create havoc in sensitive Pisceans.

Activating liver energy will **purify your blood** and enhance its vibration since liver energy is directly linked to the blood's vibration—the bridge between your Soul and your body!

A healthy liver energy will bestow you with a healthy lymphatic system—and when Pisceans do fall ill, the most important thing for them to do is increase their lymphatic system by activating liver energy, walking in the fresh air, taking deep breaths, drinking lots of spring water, and maybe spoiling yourself with a lymphatic drainage massage.

Liver flow is known as **THE number one regeneration flow!** enabling you to regenerate even after long and heavy dis-ease.

And speaking of such, it is also known as one of the most effective **beauty flows** giving you a rosy complexion and a youthful skin appearance without wrinkles!

Exhaustion and "appearing older than you are" are the results of a sluggish liver energy and can be completely transformed by activating and healing your liver energy. Liver energy enhances flexibility in both your thinking and your physical movements and has a direct connection to your **tendons** and **joints**.

Furthermore, caring for your liver energy is the best prevention against any kind of **addiction.**

An addiction is a "search"—which can be seen from the word itself in German. Addiction in German is "Sucht," which is derived from the verb "to search."

In order to be able "to search," you need to be able to SEE properly, and liver energy is an amazing energizer for your **eyes**—the reason found in its flowpath as you can see from the graphic on pages 98–99.

The liver flow, to sum it up, is the number one flow for whenever life has "hit you" in a way you thought you could not take. It enables you to "rise from the cross," from the tomb of the dead so-to-speak. It increases **consciousness,** which is also thanks to energy lock number 4, the start for the liver flow, as you will see. Energy lock number 4 is known as the "window to consciousness"—it is the place where the ancients believed the Soul leaves the body upon death and the place where consciousness enters your body again after you lost it.

Activate the liver energy and FEEL and SEE the difference it will make to your LIFE!

# Flowpath of Liver Energy

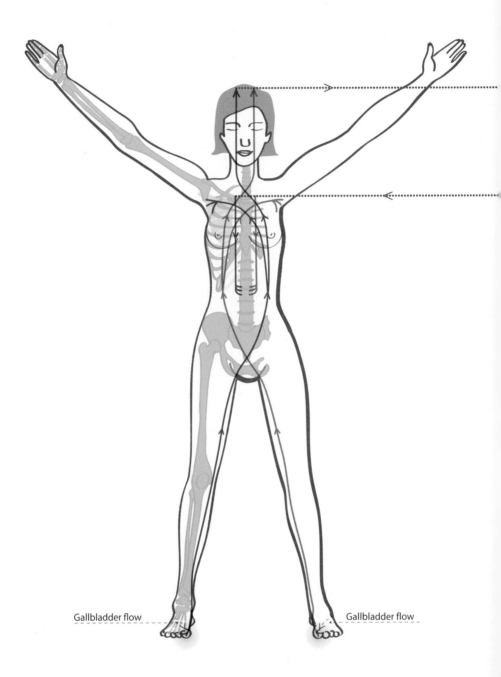

Gallbladder flow

Gallbladder flow

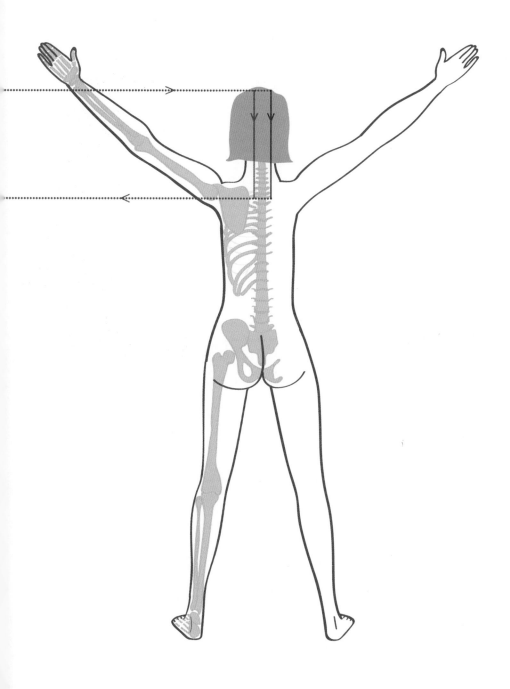

# Activating the Pisces Energy Flow
## Liver Function Energy

**Left side:** (to treat another person, sit on her right side)

Place the fingers of your left hand on your left energy lock number 4 and the fingers of your right hand on your right energy lock number 22. Keep this position for at least five minutes[1] or until you feel the energy pulsing under your fingers and flowing in your body.

**Right side:** Simply reverse the sequence (to treat another person sit on her left side).

Place the fingers of your right hand on your right energy lock number 4 and the fingers of your left hand on your left energy lock number 22. Keep this position for at least five minutes or until you feel the energy pulsing under your fingers and beginning to flow in your body.

Left Activation Liver Energy

# The Opposition of Liver Function Energy
# and How They Cooperate

Virgo's small intestine function is the opposition force of your liver energy. How do they cooperate? Well . . . let's first have a look at where Virgo's Soul Gate is located. As you can see from the diagram on page 31, Virgo's Soul Gate is located at the Third eye chakra. In fact, it IS the third eye.

Now remember the Pisces attributes we just talked about in this chapter. Liver energy is an eye energizer because its flowpath goes right through the eyes, energizing them from deep within and continuing to the brain to understand what your eyes see.

Liver energy thus energizes the eyes on a mostly physical level . . . on its flowpath. Virgo, on the other hand, has its connection to the eyes on a more spiritual level— on the level of the chakras, which energetically come "before" the organ flows. Opening Virgo's third eye increases clairvoyance—and lets you UNDERSTAND reality from a higher perspective.

In combination with Pisces liver energy, you get "the whole program": the physical as well as the spiritual level. It's all about the eyes—about being able to *see* and *feel* the energies surrounding you . . . the energies striving for manifestation—the energies that you are about to form and manifest.

Liver and small intestine cooperation, however, is not just about the eyes. It is also about keeping the blood clean and healthy and about deacidifying your body. Your body needs to be alkaline in order for you to be healthy, and liver and small intestine energies are—along with kidney energy—the main organs to keep this essential balance or to restore an alkaline level within your system.

To enhance the cooperation of liver and small intestine function energy, simply add the activation sequence of small intestine function energy to your activation program when the moon is opening the gate of Pisces.

# General Tips and Facts for
## PISCES DAYS

**Massaging the Soul Gate:**

Your Pisces Soul Gate is located at the **first vertebrae of sacrum** and should be gently massaged in the morning (ideally after taking a shower) when the moon resides in Pisces.

To do this, simply dip your fingers into some extra virgin oil (for example almond or olive oil) and then massage your Soul Gate at the sacrum by gently moving the fingers clockwise.

While doing this, imagine your **Pisces Soul Gate**, as well as the whole area around the sacrum in beautifully radiant azure-purple, the color of Pisces. Imagine your Pisces gate opening and the energy of source streaming in through it.

**Music/musical key:**

**H Major** is Pisces musical key—it is a musical key that you find and hear relatively seldom. Brahms trio in H Major is a beautiful example of H Major. Listen to this or other musical pieces in this key, and HEAR the melancholic aura that so often can be found in Pisceans. H Major has a completely different energy to its predecessor A Major—hear and *feel* the difference for yourself!

Discover **vibration** through every aspect of your LIFE!

**Physical exercise:**

To see my suggestions for physical exercise on Pisces days, go see my tips for 3rd Depth in the previous chapter. They are about 3rd Depth, and 3rd Depth—as you know—includes Aquarius as well as Pisces.

**Last but not least:**

Pisces days have a certain ethereal quality about them. You may feel "uplifted" or overly emotional. Nature may show itself either from its "wild" side with rising winds and even storms, and/or give you the most beautiful "un-real" ethereal sunsets in the evening, sunsets that let you guess—or rather BELIEVE—the truth hidden behind reality. Remember that 3rd Depth is the Depth that comes closest to God. It is the first point-of-star to rise from 6th Depth, your personal source. It is the bridge to incarnation. As such, it is not fully incarnated . . . and THIS you can feel, especially on Pisces days. Pisces days are great to visit holy places and churches. I personally remember a visit I took to the famous French Cathedral Chartres with my mother and daughter on a day when the moon was residing in Pisces. It was exceptionally beautiful and very, very spiritual. When my mother returned some time later the moon was in another sign and my mother told me that the experience was totally different—much less "holy" and spiritual.

So, discover for yourself the difference the moon can make to virtually EVERYTHING in your life! Live, think, and act according to the moon, become the moon's child, which in reality you already are and have always been!

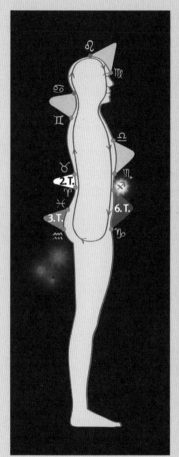
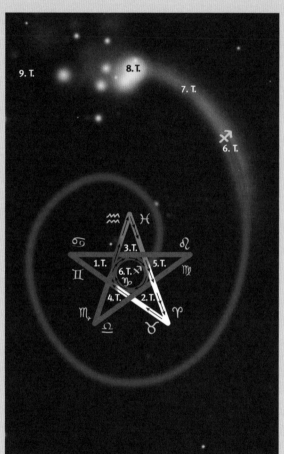

# 2nd Depth—White Point-of-Star
## AIR

The MOON Travels through the 2nd Depth
and Opens the Cosmic Gate of ARIES followed
by the Cosmic Gate of TAURUS

For you this means that you reach SOURCE by opening your . . .

## ARIES Soul Gate *through* the Vibration
## of LUNG Function Energy

followed by your . . .

## TAURUS Soul Gate *through* the Vibration
## of LARGE INTESTINE Function Energy!

# 2nd Depth—
## COURAGE to CHANGE!

**Air** is the element that follows Quintessence. Air is the mediator between the spiritual and the physical level. It is the carrier of "spirit." It is your intellect.

In Tarot, the element Air is symbolized by Swords, and in the far-east-Asian philosophy, the symbol for air is a sword!

It is the sword of intellect, cutting through illusion, trying to reason your existence.

BREATH is your tool to use this element—and so the first Soul Gate you open in this Depth is the gate of Aries.

It is the energy of taking on new—of having the COURAGE to let go of old belief systems and strive for new experiences. It is letting go of fear, the negative emotion of 4th Depth, the opposition energy of 2nd Depth, and instead TRUSTING your inner wisdom and your spirit to simply let it happen . . . to let it flow, to let your personal breath become ONE with the universal breath of the universe—

BREATH—that which initiates manifestation . . . and which keeps it going, since it is the eternal IN and OUT, UP and DOWN of BREATH that enables CREATION!

Thinking and breathing are inseparably linked—try it out for yourself next time you try to come up with a "great idea." Send out the wish to come up with a great idea. Then "forget" about it.

Relax, take a few steps, walk around the block, and concentrate on your breath —let it flow . . . take deep breaths in, and concentrate especially on breathing out. Walk for a few minutes, and let your breath do the job for you.

Upon return wait and receive . . .

Interestingly, the German word for "thought," *Gedanke,* contains in itself the syllable DANKE, which means *thank you.*

Isn't it fascinating? The words date back to our far ancestors, who had a much closer relationship to nature and to their inner wisdom. They sensed and received wisdom and accepted it—without letting intellect interfere or spoil it.

Activating 2nd Depth through lung function energy followed by large intestine function energy enables you to do the same—it enables you to let go of belief systems that have become "out of date" for you and receive the new that serve you at this very moment.

It enables you to *communicate* with your Higher Self and communicate in general. A healthy 2nd Depth is the key to a healthy communication—a giving and receiving without prejudices.

Giving and receiving in harmony—or, to put it in other words, a healthy 2nd Depth, is the best **protection against insects and parasites** who will only bother you if you "allow" them to bother you—by not caring for your 2nd Depths, your lung and large intestine function energy.

And—speaking of parasites . . . have you ever wondered why the subject of head lice predominantly appears in youngsters between the age of nine and thirteen? Well, the answer can be found—just like anything—within the Depths of your Soul, since, as you can see from table II on page 37 the ages from nine to ten are the times when Aries governs your life, with Taurus time following until the age of thirteen.

During this time, second-Depth symptoms, such as skin problems (acne) or lung problems (lungs are communication, often a difficult subject for children in prepuberty and puberty) or head lice may appear more often.

Harmonizing 2nd Depth in both the child AND the parent is the key to living this time in harmony and without distress. Generally, whenever a child has a "problem," parents should also harmonize themselves energetically, since very often the children actually bring parent problems to the surface by displaying symptoms themselves.

Harmonize 2nd Depth and BE the COURAGE to BE CHANGE!

# Harmonizing the 2nd Depth
## Ring Finger

The "quickie method" of harmonizing 2nd Depth is the ring finger. Whenever the moon passes the white area on the zodiac, your ring finger is the finger that will harmonize your whole being by activating the flow of BREATH and thus connecting you to Source.

Holding your ring finger harmonizes your 2nd Depth organs as well as a multitude of body functions (remember that each finger harmonizes 14,400 body functions). The ring finger also has a direct link to your heart through its connection to diaphragm and umbilicus function energy, as you can see from their respective flowpaths.

Wrap the fingers of your left hand around the ring finger of your right hand and keep this position for a few minutes. (Ideally for twenty minutes, but even holding it for only three minutes already has a positive effect on your body functions and emotion).

Then change hands and wrap the fingers of your right hand around your left ring finger. Again keep this position for at least three to five minutes, ideally for twenty minutes.

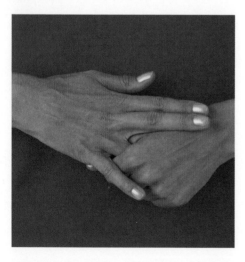

An alternative for holding your ring finger is this 2nd Depth mudra, with *mudra* being an ancient Sanscrit word meaning "that which brings happiness." It can even be used while jogging and will greatly enhance your vitality since it increases the flow of oxygen to your lungs.

Place your right thumb onto your right ring finger nail. You can do the same thing simultaneously on your left side, placing the left thumb onto the left ring finger nail.

Do this wonderfully calming yet vitalizing mudra any time you don't need your hands—and feel the difference it makes while, for example, climbing stairs. Climbing stairs will be easier—AND you will have an even more positive effect on your circulation system.

# General Tips for the Moon's Journey through the 2nd Depth

- 2nd Depth days are about rising early, since lying in bed too long during 2nd Depth days is actually harmful to your lungs and thus to your vitality.

Have you ever noticed that in times when you have a cold or a heavy cough you tend to wake up early in the morning, around 4 a.m.? Why is that? Again, have a look at table II, showing the relations of the 12 cosmic/Soul forces to the time, age, musicals keys, etc.

Lung time is between four and six o'clock, which practically means that if you do have a problem with your lungs not only are you likely to wake up at this time but also any remedy you take for your lungs at this time will have a greater effect on the lungs and your body as a whole.

Doing 2nd Depth flows at this time and/or outdoor sports or exercises (doing the sun greet of Yoga, facing the sun with the sun rising) is a fantastic lung tonic and 2nd Depth stimulizer.

Consciously inhale the sun's early morning light deep into your lungs—according to Indian Ayurvedic medicine, this is considered a fantastic lung tonic.

- Dry brush massages and sauna are a great way to increase the detoxification of your deep tissue already stimulated by the energetic activation of your 2nd Depth. Your deep tissue stores emotional pain from the past and thus keeps it "attached to the body." Freeing yourself from the past means unlocking this "storage-place," unlocking the cells, and releasing negativity. Combining the activation of 2nd Depth with dry brush massages and sauna are perfect to purify the tissue and liberate yourself of unwanted feelings and emotions of sadness.

- **Food/taste:** Pungent is the taste for 2nd Depth and it may be that during the days of the moon's journey through 2nd Depth you may suddenly crave pungent food, such as certain cream cheeses, like Roquefort. A store manager told me once that these pungent cheeses sell much better and more frequently on certain days and it turned out to be the days the moon resides in either the cosmic gates of Aries or Taurus.

Cravings (for certain foods or tastes) or the opposite—a strong dislike for certain foods—are another sign of communication of your body and Soul. Cravings and dislikes show the need to harmonize the Depth associated with that specific taste. So, listen to your body and Soul, and tune the Depth and your body into the cosmic symphony of creation led by the moon on a daily basis. The result will be strength, vibrant health, and vitality.

These foods are specific 2nd Depth foods, meaning they act like harmonizers for that specific Depth and thus for your whole body, mostly and especially of course while the moon resides in either Aries or Taurus gates: ginger, peaches, bananas, pears, tangerines, aubergines, and duck meat.

## 2nd Depth and Emotional Growth

**Grief** is the 2nd Depth attitude, which, according to Thomas von Aquin, the great theologian and philosopher of the medieval ages, is:

> *"The emotional disharmony which creates most damage to the Soul."*

By opening your 2nd Depth gates in tune with the moon, thus opening yourself to TRUTH, you transform grief and insecurity into . . .

### COURAGE AND POSITIVITY!

Aries gate / 2nd ♈
lumbar vertebrae

# THE MOON OPENS THE COSMIC GATE OF
# ARIES

*You Open Your Aries Soul Gate through the*
*Vibration of Lung Function Energy*

### Aries says:
### "I am READY! Let's do it!"

The moon opens the cosmic gate of **Aries**, thus letting TRUTH manifest itself through the musical key of **D flat Major.** Your correspondence is Aries Soul Gate located at the 2nd lumbar vertebrae and in close proximity to the kidneys.

You may have noticed that when you had a cold or general problems with your lungs and/or sinuses, that your kidneys usually show up as well, demanding special care during those times. Kidney function energy is of vital importance to the lungs mainly due to its flowpath, which goes right through the lungs, thus cleaning and vitalizing them.

However, just as the lungs need the kidneys, so do the kidneys depend on the vitality of the lung function energy.
The reason being precisely what I just mentioned: the location of Aries Soul Gate.

As you can see, any piece of information we get about an organ flow, such as the location of the Soul Gate in terms of what organs and/or energy lock lie in its surroundings, or the flowpath, just as well as the opposition energy flow, give you hints and clear signs as to how and where the organ (flow) will be helpful and what benefits you may have from it.

Another point to always look out for is the flow-direction and where the flow starts and ends.

So, besides the actual exact flowpath, simply checking where the flow starts and ends and whether it is an ascending or descending flow may give you useful information on the flow's properties and its "character."

The lung flow is an ascending flow taking over from its predecessor in the chest, making it an **ascending chest flow.** And—since all flows starting in the same area flow to the same area in the body—the Lung flow takes the energy of its predecessor liver energy up the arms into the hands and fingers where it will then transform into Taurus's large intestine energy flow.

Aries's lung flow fills every cell of your body with vital life energy. It is the number one vitality flow and especially people with a greyish skin complexion, a weak voice, and general insecurities in life will greatly profit from the activation of this vital chest flow (chest flow since the Lung flow starts in the chest).

A healthy lung energy fills you with COURAGE, and that is one of the most important attributes to have. Anything is possible—as long as you have the courage to make it happen!

## Activating the Aries Energy Flow
## Lung Function Energy:

**Left side:** (to treat another person sit on her left side)

Place the fingers of your left hand on your left energy lock number 14 and the fingers of your right hand on your left energy lock number 22. Keep this position for at least five minutes[1] or until you feel the energy pulsing under your fingers and flowing in your body.

**Right side:** Simply reverse the sequence (to treat another person sit on her right side)

Left Activation Lung Energy

Place the fingers of your right hand on your right energy lock number 14 and the fingers of your left hand on your right energy lock number 22. Keep this position for at least five minutes or until you feel the energy pulsing under your fingers and beginning to flow in your body.

## The Opposition of Lung Function Energy and How They Cooperate

**Libra** is the opposition of **Aries**, and this means that Libra's **bladder energy** is the opposition of your **lung energy**.

What do these two flows have in common, and how do they cooperate?

Let's start by having a look at the position of the Soul Gates. Aries Soul Gate, as you know, is located at the 2nd lumbar vertebrae, and thus in close proximity to the kidneys. The kidneys, as you will see in the blue chapter, belong to 4th Depth, the water element. The other 4th Depth organ is the bladder, it is the kidney's partner organ, which means that these two organs greatly depend on each other's vitality and harmony.

So, lung function helps the bladder energy by helping the kidney functions due to the proximity of Aries Soul Gate.

Now let's have a look at Libra's Soul Gate. It is located right on the heart chakra on the chest, and the heart chakra is the most important chakra for the vitality of the lungs.

Thus, by activating your bladder energy and opening Libra's Soul Gate, you automatically help the lungs. Isn't it fascinating to look at the body and the cooperation of its organs from this perspective and see how EVERYTHING is connected and depends on the cooperation of its partner organs? Just like in "real" life—or how it *should be* in real life—since unfortunately "cooperation," or rather non-cooperation in real life shows us only too well what the result of lacking cooperation is: war, hate, and crime—and this translated onto your body means "dis-ease."

Every organ has its individual "job to do" which at the same time serves as a facilitator for other organs.

# Flowpath of Lung Energy

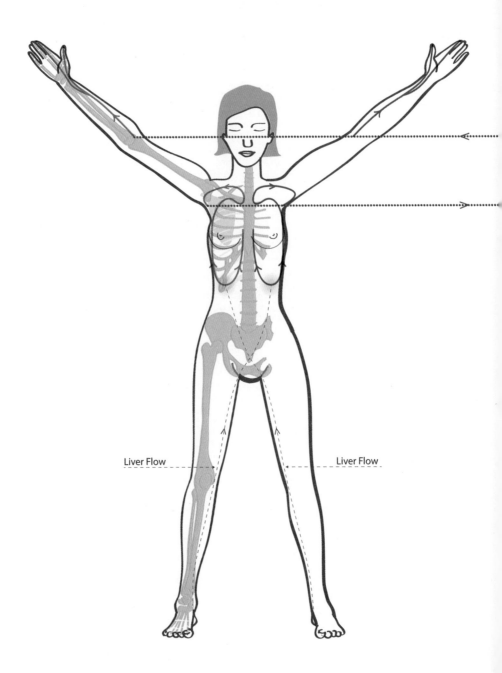

Liver Flow

Liver Flow

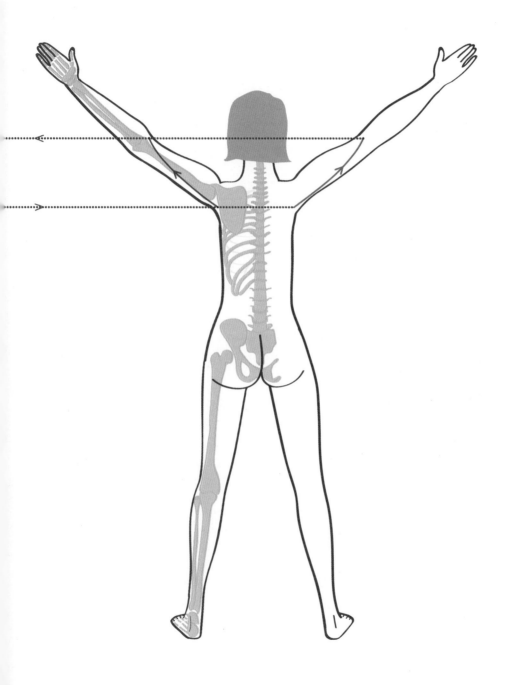

It surely will make sense to you that the best way to enhance this cooperation is by simply caring for EVERY organ in the same way—and this is precisely what you do by following the moon on a regular basis.

The moon's journey does not have any preferences on any cosmic gate but treats all 12 cosmic forces the same. Tuning into this cosmic symphony enables your body and all its organs to harmoniously play your individual melody with the vast cosmic symphony of creation.

Becoming CREATOR yourself—using all of your 12 forces—your tools for infinite creation born in heaven, are in SOURCE itself.

Both Lung and Bladder energy aid the **nervous system** and are vital for a healthy nervous system. And both flows aid in releasing old and destructive thoughts with bladder energy clearing the past on its flowpath down the back and lung energy enabling you to let go of thoughts and things no longer needed with each out breath.

Let go and BE—use your infinite potential! This is the common message of lung and bladder energy!

## General Tips and Facts for
## ARIES DAYS

**Massaging the Soul Gate:**

Your Aries Soul Gate is located at the **2nd lumbar vertebrae** and should be gently massaged in the morning (ideally after taking a shower) when the moon resides in Aries.

To do this, simply dip your fingers into some extra virgin oil (for example almond or olive oil) and then massage your Soul Gate by gently moving the fingers clockwise.

While doing this, imagine your **Aries Soul Gate**, as well as the whole kidney area in red, the color of Aries. Imagine your Aries gate opening and the energy of source streaming in through it, energizing your kidneys and your whole being!

## Music/musical key:

**D-flat Major** is the Aries musical key—it is a musical key that vibrates BREATH in the truest sense of the word. Listen to the etude "il sospiro" (the breath) by Franz Liszt; feel how it actually makes you want to take long breaths.

D-flat Major has an extremely harmonizing effect for stress situations and shock. Listen to it after a shock, and simultaneously activate both your lung function as well as its opposition bladder energy, the main organ flow for getting you centered again after shock situations.

## Physical exercise:

Aries invites you to exercise vigorously. Any outdoor sports activity is great, but especially recommended are jogging, walking, hiking, and anything that stimulates your lungs. Swimming (breast-strokes) is also perfect for Aries days and will enhance the activation of your lungs and enhance your whole vitality greatly. Aries days are great days to start a new sports regime.

## Last but not least:

Take advantage of Aries's strive for NEW and of the COURAGE that a strong lung energy will give you, and do something that you have always wanted to do but never dared to. Do it on Aries days, and the whole universe will be behind you and energize whatever you want to do.
Be the CHANGE—be the CREATOR!

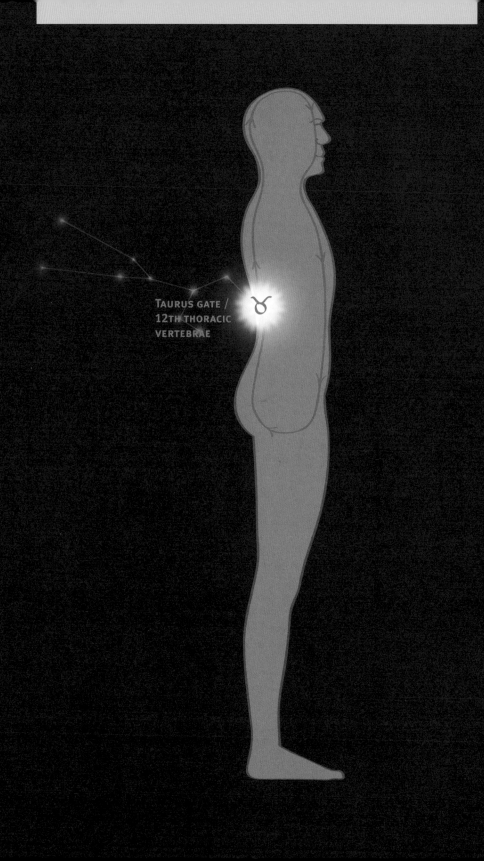

TAURUS GATE /
12TH THORACIC
VERTEBRAE

# THE MOON OPENS THE COSMIC GATE OF
# TAURUS

*You Open Your Taurus Soul Gate through the
Vibration of Large Intestine Function Energy*

**Taurus** says:
**"I have** and let go."

The cosmic (Soul) gate following Aries is the gate of Taurus. Opening Taurus's gate lets the Cosmic Symphony of creation sound in E-flat Major and thus a whole tone higher than the preceding energy of Aries.

Taurus's Soul Gate lies at the 12th thoracic vertebrae. And just as your hands, fingers, toes, and teeth are all connected to certain organs, so are your vertebraes directly linked to specific organs.

The 12th thoracic vertebrae is connected to the liver energy, and this means that by opening your Taurus gate by activating your large intestine energy, you automatically also vitalize your liver energy.

Again we see how everything is intertwined and connected with each other. **Receiving and letting go** are the big themes of Taurus and its key energy flow large intestine energy.
The large intestine flow starts in the fingers and flows down  ("down," since to show the correct flow of the organ lines the anatomical position of man needs to be with the arms and hands pointed upwards) into your face with one branch flowing down the front of your body, through the chest, and into the large intestine.

On its flowpath the large intestine flow passes through energy lock number 13—the most important energy lock for healing and to prevent major dis-ease such as breast cancer or autoimmune disorders. Activating your large intestine energy clears this vitally important energy lock with its beautiful meaning of "loving thy enemy" whereby the enemy usually is not anybody or anything exterior, but rather "interior," since we ourselves are usually our worst enemy.

Meditate on this while activating your large intestine flow, which—as you can see from its flowpath—also flows right into your gums and jaw, making it the number one **tooth and dentist flow.**

Visiting the dentist on a Taurus day is not a good idea, since on this day Taurus's large intestine flow needs all its energy to vitalize all the other organs. This, by the way, is a general rule: Generally avoid having operations or stressful procedures on organs that are currently leading the symphony of creation. So, for example, if you need an operation for your stomach, you should avoid Gemini days, since stomach energy is the key energy for the sign of Gemini.

Also: if you do need to have an operation or medical intervention, try and favor days when the moon is waning. In any case, always try to avoid full moon days for any kind of medical intervention unless it is an emergency that requires immediate attention.

Taurus days, however, are a time when your teeth my suddenly and seemingly "out of the blue" start hurting.

Usually, this pain diminishes and disappears as soon as the moon continues her journey to the following gates.

Personally, I and many others had an extreme experience this year when we had full moon in Taurus. It was a super moon, meaning the moon was very close to our planet Earth . . . closer than usual.

On those days, not only my wisdom tooth, but all of my teeth as well as my gums started hurting seemingly out of the blue in the most horrendous way—accompanied by a headache like I'd never experienced it before.

On those two to three days countless people wrote to me asking for advice for exactly the same "problem."

My advice was to activate the large intestine function energy and hold the ring finger as often and as long as possible. And simply wait until the moon leaves Taurus gate and starts waning again.

And, as if the clock stroke, as soon as the full moon in Taurus was over, the pain was gone, too.

It was the strongest moon-pain reaction I and many others had ever experienced, for the simple fact that it happened to be a so-called super-super-full moon in Taurus—the flow associated to teeth, jaw, and gums due to its flowpath.

The tooth pain was so immense, it was as if there was a super-infection. But—it was simply the large intestine flow overreacting.

These experiences show you the immense powers of the moon. A power that we—YOU—are ourselves and YOUR-self.

We always have the choice to either *use* the powers or be influenced and "used" by them.

Tuning into the moon as shown in this book on a daily basis allows you to BE the power rather than re-act to it.

To sum it up, Taurus's large intestine flow is a fantastic "dental flow," and simply holding your index finger on the opposite side of the pain (due to the flowpath of the large intestine flow, see illustrations on pages 124–125, "flowpath of large intestine energy") will help both harmonizing and clearing infections as well as against the fear since the index finger—as you will see—is the harmonizing finger of 4th Depth with its negative emotion fear and the organs bladder and kidney!

# Flowpath of Large Intestine Energy

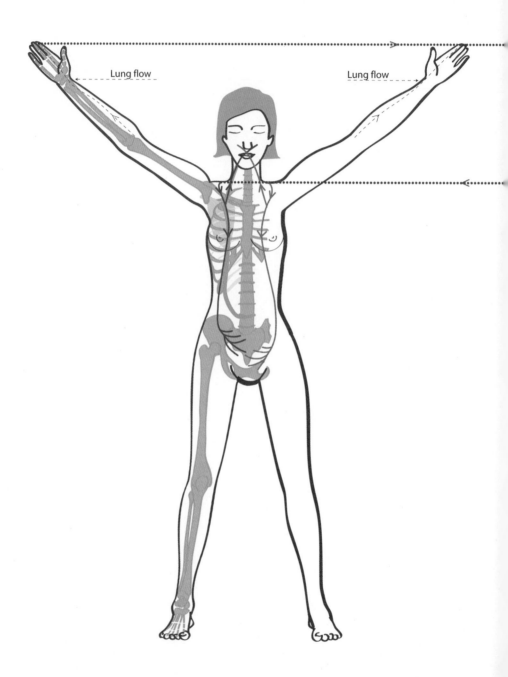

Lung flow

Lung flow

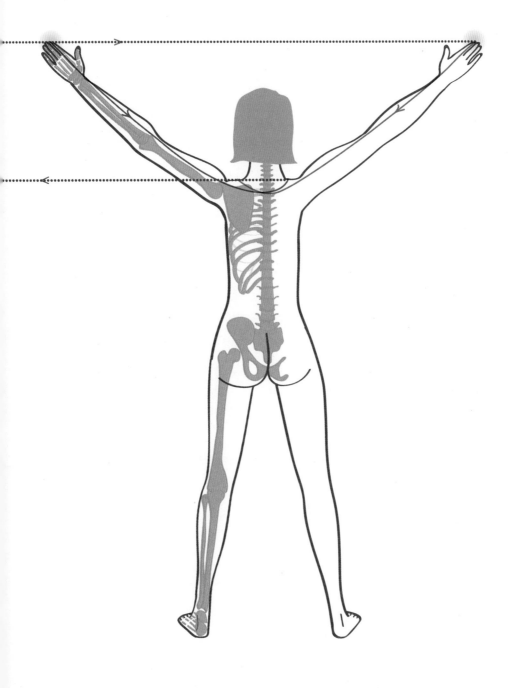

# Activating the Taurus Energy Flow
# Large Intestine Function Energy:

**Left side:** (to treat another person sit on her right side)

Place the fingers of your left hand on your right energy lock number 11, and wrap the fingers of your right hand around your left index finger. Keep this position for at least five minutes[1] or until you feel the energy pulsing under your fingers and flowing in your body.

**Right side:** Simply reverse the sequence (to treat another person sit on her left side)

Place the fingers of your right hand on your left energy lock number 11, and wrap the fingers of your left hand around your right index finger. Keep this position for at least five minutes or until you feel the energy pulsing under your fingers and beginning to flow in your body.

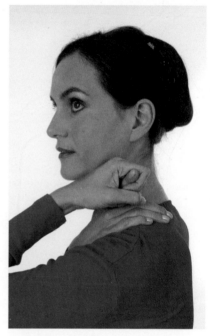

Right Activation Large Intestine Energy

## The Opposition of Large Intestine Function Energy and How They Cooperate

Kidney energy is the opposition of large intestine function energy since kidney is the organ associated with Scorpio, the opposing sign of Taurus on the Zodiac.

Kidney energy to Large intestine function energy acts like a flush, a cleansing flush aiding your large intestine energy to do exactly what it is meant to do: to cleanse and rid yourself of garbage.

Let's have a look at the location of both your Soul Gates of Scorpio as well as your Soul Gate of Large intestine: Scorpio Soul Gate lies on the solar plexus and Taurus Soul Gate is located exactly on the same level but on your back at the 12 thoracic vertebrae.

You could actually draw a line from front to back, from Scorpio to Taurus Soul Gate and be centered.

Centering and being centered is what Scorpio and Taurus Soul Gates are all about. Taking and giving and keeping the harmony between these two poles is the main attribute of Scorpio and Taurus. If you have the feeling of "being used," the harmony in either one of these two organ forces may be blocked. Activating one or both of them will help you regain your natural authority of saying NO and/or of allowing to TAKE rather than just give.

Give yourself an extra energy boost by activating kidney energy whenever the moon is residing in the gate of Taurus and be totally centered and in Peace.

## General Tips and Facts for
# TAURUS DAYS

**Massaging the Soul Gate:**

Your Taurus Soul Gate is located at the **12th thoracic vertebrae** and should be gently massaged in the morning (ideally after taking a shower) when the moon resides in Taurus.

To do this simply dip your fingers into some extra virgin oil (for example almond or olive oil) and then massage your Soul Gate by gently moving the fingers clockwise.

While doing this, imagine your **Taurus Soul Gate**, as well as the whole Solar plexus area on your back, in brown-pink, the colors of Taurus.

**Music/musical key:**

**E-flat Major** is Taurus's musical key—to reach E-flat Major from D-flat Major, Aries's Soul Gate, we climb up the cosmic musical letter a whole tone, as we have done since we started our cosmic dance at Sagittarius Soul Gate. To get to our next gate, however, to Gemini, as you will see, we will take a bigger step—a whole tone and a half, since we have reached the "turning point" where the moon will commence to descend again towards Sagittarius Soul Gate. Isn't it amazing that you can actually *hear* this through the musical tones?

**Physical exercise:**

Morning sports in the fresh air, like **walking** or **jogging,** are ideal to get your large intestine "moving" and to activate it. It will also enhance your breathing, and large intestine and the lungs are directly linked through their "mother Depth" 2nd Depth. Activating your large intestine will always also aid your breathing.

**Last but not least:**

Activating large intestine energy—especially in cooperation with kidney energy—aids in *letting go* and *regenerating* in every aspect of your life.

Take advantage of the moon's residence in Taurus gate to let go of anything you feel may hinder your spiritual and general journey in life. Let it go and allow to RECEIVE. Have confidence that the more you let go, the more abundantly you will RECEIVE directly from SOURCE!

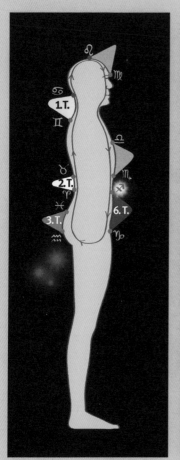

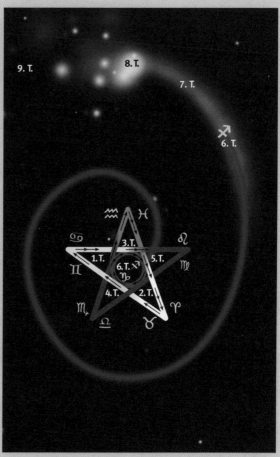

# 1st Depth—Yellow Point-of-Star
## EARTH

The MOON travels through the 1st Depth
and opens the cosmic gate of GEMINI followed
by the cosmic gate of CANCER.

For you, this means that you reach SOURCE by opening your . . .

GEMINI Soul Gate *through* the vibration
of STOMACH Function Energy,

followed by your . . .

CANCER Soul Gate *through* the vibration
of SPLEEN Function Energy!

# The YELLOW Point-of-Star and Its Element EARTH!

## Nutrition, Grounding, Manifestation!

REALIZE YOUR DREAMS could be the motto of 1st Depth—the yellow point-of-star with its beautiful bright yellow-gold light! Color of the sun!

With 1st Depth we are halfway through our cosmic journey of creation. We have reached the most physical point on our journey, the place where MANIFESTATION takes place.

Anything that needs to be realized and done within a cosmic lunar cycle should be done NOW—with the aid of the whole universe behind you.

Yellow is a beautiful bright color that gives joy by simply looking at it. It is the color associated with the sun, the heavenly body of SOURCE, healing power, and positive energy.

A strong and healthy 1st Depth will make you feel "centered and at home." It will give you this beautiful feeling of "being at home"—at home in your body—the temple of your SOUL. Activating 1st Depth **strengthens your aura and fills it with light.**

It gives you the kind of confidence that a child with a loving mother has, the feeling that everything that you need is already THERE—always and everywhere . . . a feeling of "being at the right place" and loving your body.

This is what 1st Depth is about. It is the most female of all Depths. It is the Depth that needs most nurturing whenever there is a difficult or damaged relationship with your mother or the absence of loving female persons while you were growing up.

1st Depths nurturing aspect strengthens your **nerves** and literally fills them with light. Strong nerves are the basic and the root of EVERYTHING in life. The nerves are like antennas for the energy streaming into your body from SOURCE, from 6th Depth, the opposition Depth of 1st Depth. 6th Depth provides the light from Source, and 1st Depth receives it and distributes it to all the organs and cells of your body.

1st Depth is the sun—it is the golden center of your body—and being centered is the condition for SUCCESS in our material world.

It thus does not come as a surprise that 1st Depth and the color yellow is actually connected to **money** and/or the ability to earn and keep enough material goods to make a healthy and comfortable living.

It is the Depth associated with a healthy pregnancy as well as the ability to father a child and **conceive**.

Couples wishing for a child should always strengthen their first as well as their 4th Depth with the harmony of both Depths and their interaction also being an amazing protection against cancer.

**Receiving, transformation,** and **distribution** are the main aspects of 1st Depth, and activating your 1st Depth enables you to—similar to second Depth, but with the emphasis on the receiving rather than the giving aspect—receive and USE with confidence.

1st Depth is like a big HUG—it is the motherly hug that YOU yourself can give yourself by activating and harmonizing 1st Depth—and this can be as simple as holding your thumb!

# Harmonizing the 1st Depth
## Thumb

The "quickie method" of harmonizing 1st Depth is the thumb. Whenever the moon passes the yellow area on the zodiac, your thumb is the finger that will harmonize your whole being by giving you a feeling of being centered and calm.

The thumb is in actual fact not a "finger." It is the leader of the 4 fingers following it, with the 4 being the number of manifestation. The thumb "gives the beat," so to speak, and the better you care for your thumb and its associated organs, the better all the other organs of your body will function.

Wrap the fingers of your left hand around the thumb of your right hand and keep this position for a few minutes. (Ideally for twenty minutes, but even holding it for only three minutes will have a positive effect on your body functions and emotion).

Then change hands and wrap the fingers of your right hand around your left thumb. Again keep this position for at least three to five minutes, ideally for twenty minutes.

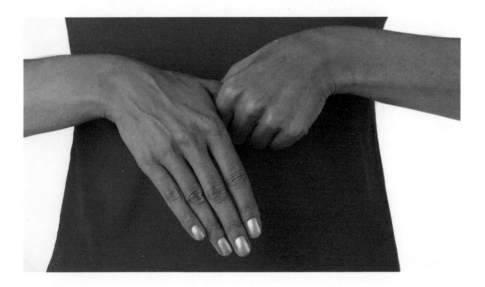

**Special advice:** While holding your thumb and/or activating your 1st Depth organs stomach and spleen energy, visualize your stomach and spleen area in the most beautiful golden yellow. FEEL this warm, uplifting color spread into your whole body from your solar plexus area, and THANK your spleen and stomach while activating them! Talk to them, and let them talk back to you. Love them, and let them love you back with RADIANT HEALTH.

## General Tips for the Moon's Journey
## through the 1st Depth

- **Sitting** for long hours weakens your 1st Depth. People working in an office should, therefore, take a break from sitting at least every hour. Stand up, move around, drink a sweet Chai Tea (natural sweetness, as you will see, strengthens 1st Depth), and of course, keep your 1st Depth strong by holding your thumb whenever the moon travels through the yellow gates, and activate your 1st Depth organs stomach and spleen energy.

Yawning is, by the way, a sign of a weak spleen energy. It is your spleen energy telling you to energize it. If you don't have time for the activation sequence, then try at least to visualize it in beautiful golden-yellow light and THANK it. This takes only a few seconds but has strong energizing effect.

- **Bright golden yellow** is the color of 1st Depth. Do you feel drawn to that color or do you have a special adversity against yellow? Both are a sure sign of your body telling you its need for 1st Depth strengthening. Yellow-up your own by adding bright, yellow, sunny touches. Wear yellow, especially of course when the moon travels through 1st Depth gates and also on Saturday, since Saturn, the 1st Depth planet, rules Saturday.

- **Rose** scent is a fantastic 1st Depth harmonizer. The scent of roses can sometimes even be smelt when you harmonize your 1st Depth. It is YOU, your 1st Depth, telling you "thank you for looking after me!"

- **Food/taste: SWEET** is the taste of 1st Depth, and in Ayurvedic food, sweet porridges and teas play a major part. Sweet, however, means natural sweetness, like honey or sweet spices. **Millet** is the number one grain to strengthen 1st Depth. Anybody with a week spleen energy, bulimic girls and people with low self-esteem, should switch to Millet as their main grain. Top it up with herbs and curcuma with its wonderful orange color—with orange being the color of umbilicus function energy, the opposition of spleen energy—and you have a tasty and very healthy, nutritious meal!

**Cherries** are the number one fruit to strengthen 1st Depth and they contain a vast amount of healthy substances, minerals, and vitamins. Eat them abundantly when they grow, but make sure it is only organic cherries you eat to avoid filling yourself with residues of pesticides.

Other great 1st Depth foods are: apples, figs, tofu, wheat, sweet potatoes, ginger, mushrooms, and sweet teas.

# 1st Depth and Emotional Growth

**Worry** is the negative emotion of 1st Depth and a sure sign that either one or both of your 1st Depth organs are out of harmony. Harmonize your 1st Depth and transform any worries into . . .

## OPENNESS AND SERENITY!

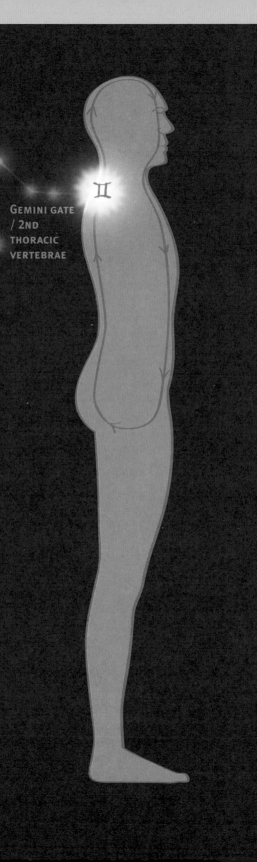

GEMINI GATE
/ 2ND
THORACIC
VERTEBRAE

# THE MOON OPENS THE COSMIC GATE OF
# GEMINI

*You Open Your Gemini Soul Gate through the
Vibration of Stomach Function Energy*

### Gemini says:
### "I think!"

The first cosmic gate that the moon opens on its voyage through 1st Depth is the gate of Gemini, which corresponds to your Gemini Soul Gate at the second thoracic vertebrae—Gemini Soul Gate through which the cosmic symphony of creation sounds in F-sharp Major, which for me means:

In order for me to be in harmony with the whole universe during the moon's stay in Gemini gate, I activate my stomach function energy, thus opening my Gemini gate and enabling the vital energy of SOURCE to pour into my being, energizing body, mind, and spirit.

Stomach function energy is a descending face-flow, taking over from its predecessor large intestine energy in the face and taking the energy down the front of your body to your feet.

It not only clears your head and your thinking (Gemini are known for their active mental mind) but also your "sins of life" sitting in the area around your energy lock number 14, just below the rib cage.

It is here, at the home of liver and spleen, that you store your disappointments—your hate, rage, and anger.

And it is here that you clear these "sins," enabling the sins to flow down the front of your body and leave your life, flowing out of your toes.

Stomach flow thus brings PEACE into a distressed life. It is the psychiatrist of your life. A psychiatrist that enables you to let go and move on, something which can even be seen from the flowpath itself.

Have a look at the flowpath of stomach function energy, pages 140–141.

Stomach energy flows right through the knees, and it is right here that movement forward takes place.

Knee problems often show us that we are at a place and time in our life where we would like to move forward but somehow don't.

The body makes us aware of this by the fact that we keep hitting our knees, for example, or even injuring them.

Knee problems are ALWAYS a reminder of moving forward. Since this is the only way there is in life—FORWARD.

Stomach flow enables you to MOVE—forward—and at the same time makes you beautiful, since the stomach flow is one of the beauty flows (although strictly speaking each flow is a "beauty flow" since health equals beauty).

However, there are certain flows that are specifically liked by men and women who prefer energy work to estheticians—and stomach flow is one of them.

On its flowpath, starting just under the eyes, it clears the eyes, making them bright and shiny, clears puffiness in the face, gives a rosy complexion, and clears wrinkles. It's a cosmetic flow in the truest sense of its word.

On its flowpath it also clears the shoulders—the place where most people store fears and rigidness. Open your shoulders and the world will be a different place—in a very, very positive way.

Change ALWAYS starts with you—and activating your organ flows is the most effective and, at the same time, easiest way to enable this change on the energy level, which is the level preceding everything.

Let's now have a look at the Soul Gate of Gemini, at the second thoracic vertebrae. It is where energy lock 3 is located, the energy lock that is also known as "the gate to the lungs."

This is why activating your stomach function energy also helps and activates your lungs—yet another example of the fascinating interaction of your organ functions, the Soul Gates, and the energy locks.

Wisdom and cosmic creative power, which YOU yourself ARE.

Let your body speak to you—through its organs, its Soul Gates, its energy locks, and any part of the body—since any part of your body can and does give you special hints to yourself.

It is up to YOU to listen to the voice of your SOUL and act accordingly.

## Activating the Gemini Energy Flow
## Stomach Function Energy

**Left side:** (to treat another person sit on her left side)

Place the fingers of your right hand on your left energy lock number 21 and the fingers of your left hand on your left energy lock number 22. Keep this position for at least five minutes[1] or until you feel the energy pulsing under your fingers and flowing in your body.

**Right side:** Simply reverse the sequence (to treat another person sit on her right side)

Place the fingers of your left hand on your right energy lock number 21 and the fingers of your right hand on your right energy lock number 22. Keep this position for at least five minutes or until you feel the energy pulsing under your fingers and beginning to flow in your body.

Left Activation Stomach Energy

# Flowpath of Stomach Energy

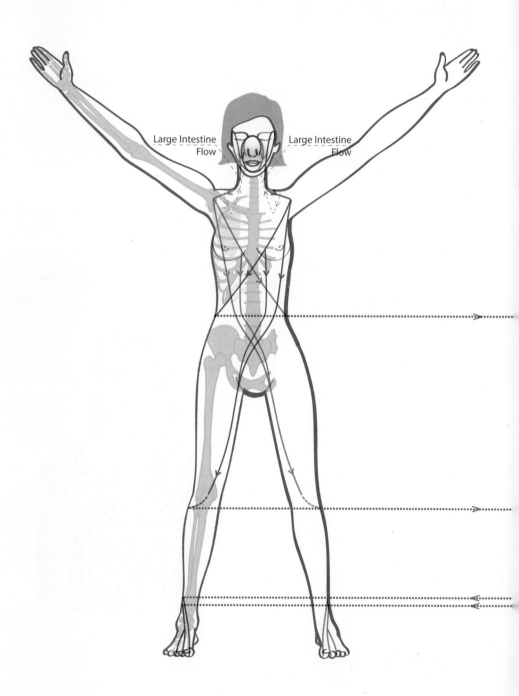

Large Intestine Flow

Large Intestine Flow

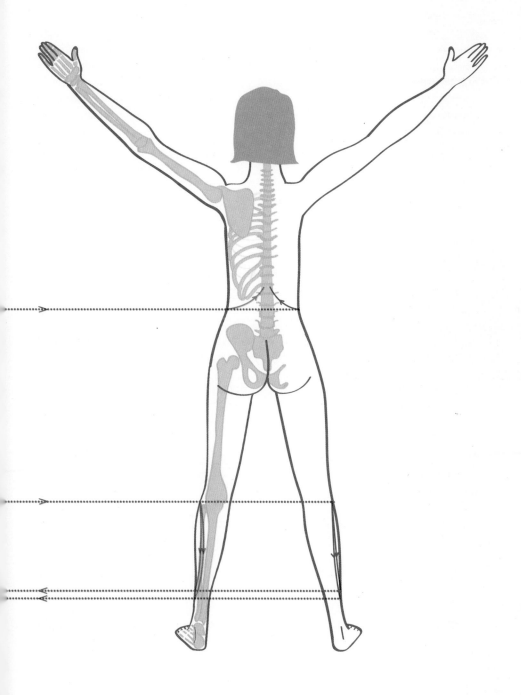

# The Opposition of Stomach Function Energy and How They Cooperate

The opposition of Gemini is Sagittarius, meaning the Sagittarius flow diaphragm function energy is the "helper-flow" of stomach energy. We spoke about this opposition already in our Sagittarius chapter at "The opposition of diaphragm energy and how they cooperate," page 62. To give your stomach energy an extra boost, simply add the activation sequence of diaphragm energy, thus enabling the ascending (diaphragm) and descending (stomach) energy to truly cooperate for the best of your HEALTH.

# General Tips and Facts for Gemini Days

**Massaging the Soul Gate:**

Your Gemini Soul Gate is located at the **second thoracic vertebrae** and should be gently massaged in the morning (ideally after taking a shower) when the moon resides in Gemini.

To do this, simply dip your fingers into some extra virgin oil (for example almond or olive oil) and then massage your Soul Gate by gently moving the fingers clockwise.

While doing this, imagine your **Gemini Soul Gate** in a soft yellow-sky blue color, the color of Gemini.

**Music/musical key:**

**F-sharp Major** is Gemini's musical key—one and a half tones up from its predecessor musical key E-flat Major!

With this, the moon is showing you that she started her descent again—the descent towards Sagittarius gate, the opposition of Gemini.

Sagittarius and Gemini are the two "breaking points" along the eternal cosmic creative symphony. USE this knowledge to speed up things you have left undone so far within this cosmic cycle. Activate your stomach function energy and listen to a musical peace in F-sharp Major, while imagining your stomach energy in bright yellow, thanking it for its work.

**Physical exercise:**

Gemini days are days of movement, but take care not to overdo it. Gemini days may overstimulate your nerves, so you should counteract by doing calming and centering exercises like **meditation** or **Qi gong.**

**Last but not least:**

Gemini days are like the Geminis themselves: mentally active and very changeable days, changeable meaning, for example, that the weather on Gemini days may abruptly change from sun to rain or vice versa— just like the nature of Gemini. Use the mental energy given to you by the universe and the moon, and schedule a visit to an interesting museum, or—if you are a lecturer—give your talk on a Gemini day. People will be specifically interested on these days, even if they may forget the information quicker than on other days.

That is if they haven't activated their stomach energy before. If you do give a lecture or talk on Gemini days, ask your audience to hold their thumb while you speak— it will allow your information to be absorbed much better and at the same time create an amazing energy of calmness and harmony.

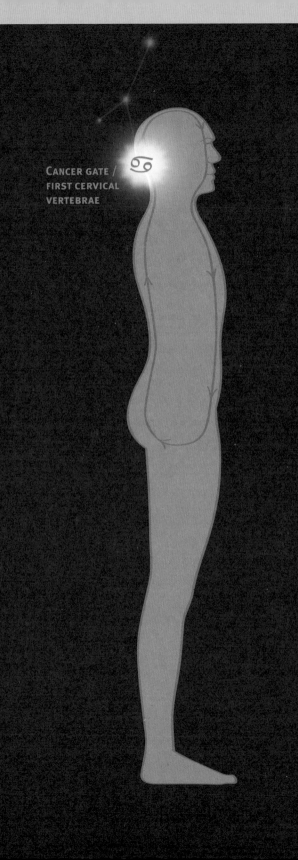

CANCER GATE /
FIRST CERVICAL
VERTEBRAE

⊚

# THE MOON OPENS THE COSMIC GATE OF
# **CANCER**

*You Open your Cancer Soul Gate through the
Vibration of Spleen Function Energy*

### **Cancer** says:
### "I feel!"

The second gate, which the moon opens within the yellow point-of-star, the 1st
Depth, is the cosmic gate of Cancer. By opening the gate of Cancer the moon lets
the cosmic symphony sound in G-sharp Major—a very special musical key indeed.
Special, since G-sharp is actually the tone of the MOON.

If you could *hear* the moon, you would hear G-sharp, and G-sharp is considered
the tone that even people with a perfect musical ear have the greatest difficulty
hearing—just like the Soul, the human counterpart of the moon, for most humans
is the most difficult "thing" to "grasp," understand, or even acknowledge.

The key to open the gate of cancer is the spleen function energy—the organ function
that in Asian philosophy and medicine is considered the most important centering
organ function of the body.

Being the organ of the moon, the spleen acts like a distributor—distributing the
light from nutrition to all the organs and cells of the body.

Spleen is of vital importance for the **immune system** and the proper functioning
of the **nerves** and the **nervous system**.

In traditional Far East Asian medicine the spleen is considered an organ function
of vital importance for its task of supplying the "light drawn out of the food you
eat" to the cells of your body.

So, just as the sun needs the moon to transform the light—to make it usable for
creation so to speak, so does the spleen act as a food-transformer.

And, just like the sun is associated with success, self-confidence, and warmth, so is the spleen energy known as the number one energy for **Earthly success!**

As we have heard already when discussing 1st Depth as a whole, **yellow** is known as the color of money. If you feel you could be doing better in this aspect or if your confidence could need a boost, pay special attention to the activation of your spleen. Imagine it in bright yellow, like a sun. While activating your spleen or holding your thumb THANK your spleen—both mentally as well as verbally—for its beautiful light and its important work; feel into your spleen. LOVE your spleen and BE your spleen!

After a few seconds you will feel your spleen responding—you may feel warmth emanating from just below your left rib cage.

You can do this exercise any time of day—ideally, however, it is done in the morning before getting up or at spleen time between ten and twelve o'clock a.m. Do it while either doing the activation sequence and/or while holding your thumb. Or—for a real quickie in between—simply give your spleen a quick loving thought in between, thanking it for its beautiful, radiant yellow light!

I am just noticing that as I am writing these lines it actually is the spleen time and so I am giving my spleen some loving thoughts with instant positive reaction!

The spleen—along with the kidney energy—are the only organ function energies I would actually suggest to do daily, on top of your daily Moon Flow and the Life Flow. They are of such vital importance and are also dysfunctional in the majority of people—I highly recommend taking them as basic flows—just like the Life Flow, which should be your essential daily flow—your daily connection to your personal source!

Due to its special connection to the breast, the spleen flow is also known as the "female" flow—forming, nourishing, and protecting the female breast. Spleen is of vital importance in the prevention of breast cancer.

However, spleen does not only protect against breast cancer—and aid in the healing process in women who are affected—it is generally one of the main **anti-cancer flows.**

And, just like with all the other flows, looking at the flowpath already gives us information on which symptoms may be linked to the energy flow.

So, have a look at the flowpath of the spleen flow, pages 148–149 starting from the big toe. (Yes, toenail problems are linked to spleen, specifically of the right foot, since the energy crosses over to the other side of the body at the hip. Toenail problems of the left foot tend to imply liver problems.) It flows up the leg, crosses over at the pubic bone, energizes the reproductive organs, and then flows to the heart and the breast.

It comes as no surprise that Hildegard von Bingen, a mystic saint from the medieval ages in Germany, already then said that "the spleen cleanses the heart."

The harmony and vitality of the spleen is of vital importance for the heart, for the fire element of your body. It is like a vessel containing the fire so that it does not burn you.

The spleen is the female organ of your body with the liver incorporating the male aspect.

Practically, this means that especially problems with the mother or the mother aspect show in this energy AND of course can be healed by it.

The spleen energy is like "a motherly embrace," supplying you the warmth and security (security is linked to the Earth element) you may have lacked from your mother in your youth.

The spleen is the most important organ function energy in the prevention of and cure of **diabetes**—one of the most common dis-eases of our times.

It is the inability to enjoy "the sweetness of your life"—to nurture yourself.

Activating your spleen energy does just that for you: it NURTURES and COMFORTS you.

Activate your spleen energy and BE the SUN of your LIFE.

# Flowpath of Spleen Energy

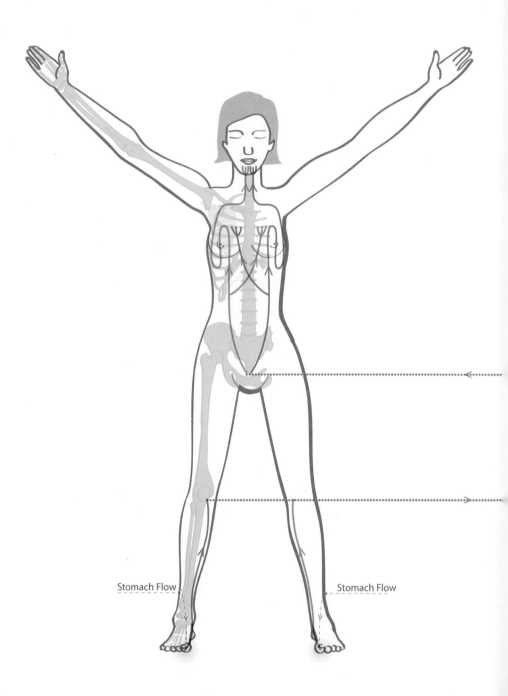

Stomach Flow

Stomach Flow

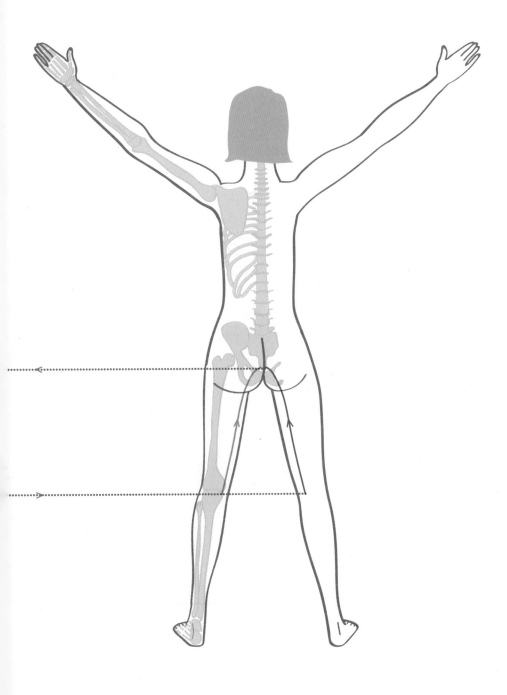

# Activating the Cancer Energy Flow
## Spleen Function Energy

**Left side:** (to treat another person sit on her left side)

Place the fingers of your left hand on your left energy lock number 5, and simply slip your right hand under your coccyx. Keep this position for at least five minutes or until you feel the energy pulsing under your fingers and beginning to flow in your body.

**Right side:** Simply reverse the sequence (to treat another person sit on her right side)

Place the fingers of your right hand on your right energy lock number 5, and slip your left hand under your coccyx. Keep this position for at least five minutes or until you feel the energy pulsing under your fingers and beginning to flow in your body.

Right Activation Spleen Energy

## The Opposition of Spleen Function Energy
## and How They Cooperate

The opposition of Cancer is Capricorn, meaning the Capricorn flow umbilicus function energy is the "helper-flow" of spleen energy.

These two flows are the main organ flows to prevent and heal autoimmune disorders. Their cooperation is also of vital importance for the immune system. They are like the police (umbilicus flow) and the psychologist (spleen flow), keeping your body in harmony and connected to Source.

We spoke about the cooperation of spleen and umbilicus function energy already in our Umbilicus function chapter, "The Opposition of Umbilicus Energy and How They Cooperate," page 72. To give your spleen energy an extra boost simply add the activation of umbilicus energy, thus enabling the ascending (spleen) and descending (umbilicus) energy to truly cooperate for YOU!

# General Tips and Facts for
# Spleen Days

**Massaging the Soul Gate:**

Your Cancer Soul Gate is located at the **first cervical vertebrae** and should be gently massaged in the morning (ideally after taking a shower) when the moon resides in cancer.

To do this, simply dip your fingers into some extra virgin oil (for example, almond or olive oil) and then massage your Soul Gate by gently moving the fingers clockwise.

While doing this imagine your **Cancer Soul Gate** in silver, the color of both the moon and cancer!

**Music/musical key:**

**G-sharp Major** is the musical key of cancer—one full tone up from its predecessor Gemini, which sounds in F-sharp Major.

With hardly any compositions available in this Soul tone, my suggestion is to listen to the vibration of the moon, which corresponds to the tone G-sharp. Or . . . listen to compositions played by orchestras tuned into G-sharp instead of the current chamber tone A. Mozart's tuning fork was actually tuned to a vibration corresponding to the tone of the moon. With the current much higher, tuning compositions have a different effect. They lack in Soul. Try to find your favorite composition with a lower tuning—ideally corresponding to G-sharp—and feel the effect it has on your Soul. It is amazing!

**Physical exercise:**

Cancer days are days to relax and get comfy with your loved ones. During cancer days it is not unusual to be wet and foggy, which also makes these days perfect for a wellness day in the spa. Why not take a whole day off? Spend it in the spa, also enjoying a nice massage, and end the day with a candlelight dinner with your loved one at home or in your favorite restaurant.

**Last but not least:**

Use cancer days to connect consciously with both yourSELF and your loved ones. Cancer is the sign of consciousness. Becoming conscious of who you really are is essential for any relationship you have with other people.

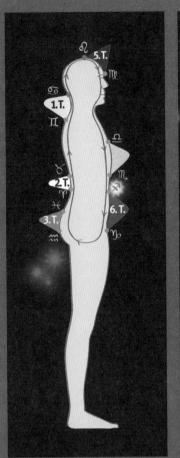

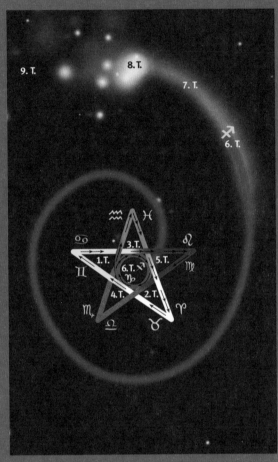

# 5th Depth—Red Point-of-Star
## FIRE

The MOON travels through the 5th Depth
and opens the cosmic gate of LEO followed
by the cosmic gate of VIRGO.

For you, this means that you reach SOURCE by opening your . . .

## LEO Soul Gate *through* the vibration of HEART Function Energy,

followed by your . . .

## VIRGO Soul Gate *through* the vibration of SMALL INTESTINE Function Energy!

# The RED Point-of-Star and Its Element FIRE!
## LOVE, Passion, Ecstasy!

Red, the color of LOVE and the color of power, strength, and—at times—aggression!

**Mars** is the planet of 5th Depth—it is the planet also associated with war and impulsiveness.

However, Mars also is and remains the planet of deep spiritual love—coming from the heart, the seat of Spirit.

True, spiritual love rises above Earthly desires and sexuality. In fact, true love is born deep within the spiritual centers of man. It is the feeling of complete ONEness—a sense of BEING SOURCE yourself . . . a sense of abundance that cannot be topped by anything material or physical.

True love does not know jealousy or fear of losing someone—since true, spiritual love is the product of UNITY—meaning the deep knowledge that we are all ONE. You cannot "lose" something you already are—within your energy, you (we)—are all one at all times.

Nowhere else can the difficult relationship of "water"(fear) and "fire"(spiritual ecstasy) be seen and experienced clearer than in love relationships. The fear of losing your partner is in reality the result of being disconnected from Source—with the direct result of "missing something," of not "having enough."

Water, the element of 4th Depth, the blue point-of-star, will extinguish the fire of spiritual love, the red point-of-star, if the water becomes too strong.

The water needs to be contained by a vessel, by the element Earth, represented specifically by the spleen energy, the yellow point-of-star about which you learned in the last chapter.

A weak spleen energy leaves you worrying—a weak kidney energy leaves you fearful—LOVE is able to cure both; however, a strong and harmonious cooperation of kidney and spleen will enable love on the other hand.

This shows how everything in life is connected to the harmonious cooperation of your organ functions—the tools of your Soul.

Love your organs—the tools of your Soul—and they will not only love you back but also enable you to truly, deeply, and spiritually LOVE—in the very sense of its word.

5th Depth, the red point-of-star, is your gate to heaven here on Earth—live and BE the red point-of-star, and love will cure your life from within!

# Harmonizing the 5th Depth
## Little Finger

The "quickie method" of harmonizing fifth Depth is the pinkie. Whenever the moon passes the dark red area on the zodiac, your pinkie is the finger that will harmonize and energize your whole being within minutes.

The little finger can be lifesaving. I remember taking a first-aid class some years ago with a highly respected emergency doctor teaching us. In his own words he said than when someone has a heart attack and "nothing else helps," try holding the patients left pinkie, or even biting in the nail of the left small finger.

Funnily, he did not know "why"—but he said this "trick" brought back the majority of patients.

I myself experienced the saving of several patients' lives by simply holding their little fingers when they collapsed. I had only just started to learn about energy healing when it happened to my mother—she collapsed after arriving in the Tropics from the cold, European winter. I asked my then four-year-old daughter to hold one little finger as I held the other one while taking the cab to see the emergency doctor. My mother was in a critical situation; however, after only a few minutes of holding the pinkie, the color returned to her face and she "came back to us." When we arrived at the doctors, she again was perfectly fine.

Wrap the fingers of your left hand around the little finger of your right hand and keep this position for a few minutes. (Ideally for twenty minutes, but even holding it for only three minutes already has a positive effect on your body functions and emotion.)

Then change hands and wrap the fingers of your right hand around your left pinkie. Again keep this position for at least three to five minutes, ideally for twenty minutes.

Imagine your heart in a beautiful bright red light—imagine it as a blossoming flower—emanating a beautiful perfume and radiating LOVE. LOVE your heart, and it will love you back and enable YOU to truly LOVE!

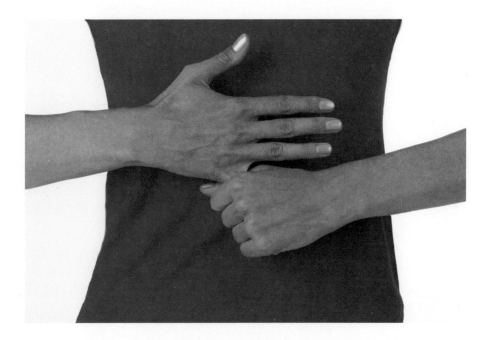

## Journey through the 5th Depth

- Physical exercise is important and promotes wellbeing. However—when the moon travels through 5th Depth you should not overdo sport and not start a new sport regime. Walking too much strains your heart and small intestine energies, so if you have a heart problem and the moon passes 5th Depth, hold your pinkie instead, and enjoy an amazing circulation. The pinkie on another level opens energy lock 23, which is the main energy lock for the water element and for circulation, so by holding your pinkie you increase your circulation as if you had done physical sport.

- **Red** is the color of 5th Depth. Do you feel drawn to that color or do you have a special adversity against red? Red is the color of love and energy. Energize your life by wearing red specifically when the moon travels through 5th Depth.

- **Food/taste: BITTER** food is an amazing 5th Depth harmonizer and strengthener. Bitter is the taste that is lacking in most American and western diets. Try to eat more bitter foods, like for example, dandelion salad or drink olive leaves tea—your heart will love you for it!

Lemon juice can be seen both as a bitter and as a sour taste—thus harmonizing both 3rd and 5th Depth which, as you know, are opposition Depths anyway.

# Fifth Depth and Emotional Growth

**Pretense**—trying to be something you are not is the negative emotion of 5th Depth. In fact, managers who practically live for their company, giving up their true spiritual identity, are more likely to suffer from heart attacks than someone living and being his/her true self, the TRUTH. Harmonize your 5th Depth and transform pretense into . . .

## HAPPINESS, LOVE, PASSION, and HONESTY!

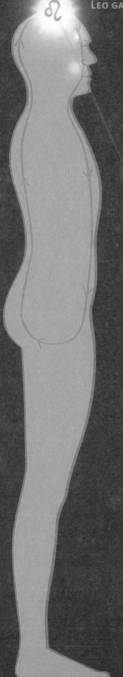

LEO GATE / TOP OF HEAD

# THE MOON OPENS THE COSMIC GATE OF
# LEO

*You Open Your Leo Soul Gate through the*
*Vibration of Heart Function Energy*

### Leo says:
### "I radiate LOVE!"

The spleen flow becomes the heart flow in the chest . . . or—to put it in other words—feeling centered, secure, and in harmony with yourself (spleen energy) evolves into pure LOVE—love that is carried from the heart, the seat of Spirit, to your hands, carried to your hands for you to *use* this highest of all positive emotions and *create* out of it.

Anything that is created out of love will always be god-like—HAS to be god-like since LOVE *is* deep religiousness—with religious not being attached to a certain religion but meaning what it actually means: to be connected = to be ONE. (Latin religion = reverence for the gods).

If we could physically "hear" the heart energy, we would hear a melody in A-sharp Major—a musical key just as rare to find in musical compositions as spleen's G-sharp Major.

Isn't it a strange paradox that MAN has the greatest difficulties hearing, identifying, and indeed accepting exactly that which is—in the truest sense of its word—the heart of everything?

That man has the greatest difficulties with exactly that which he longs for most?

Activating your heart flow will get you in touch with your SELF and live exactly what you long for most—the powerful emotion of pure love which—as we have already heard—vibrates in a much higher frequency than the physical love we often mistake for "the real thing."

Activating your heart flow with the activation sequence shown further down will strengthen your heart energy in a way that will make you *see* the truth behind the veil of illusion.

Seeing, accepting, believing, and living your truth in the end is the best and only key to eternal bliss and perfect health.

It thus does, as no surprise that the heart flow also **strengthens the physical eyes**— on its flowpath through the eyes.

If you have a look at the flowpath graphic of the heart flow on pages 164–165 you will see that the heart—after passing the eyes—continues right into the **brain.**

This shows the strong connection of the heart energy to the brain and anything connected to it: Alzheimer's disease, for example, has a strong connection to the heart as has the **memory** (on Leo days people often do not remember things as well or/and even suddenly stutter).

A strong heart energy lets you shine and be the center of attraction—without even having to do anything for it except of course caring for your heart energy.

Just think of a Lion with its beautiful mane—which in fact brings us to another one of heart energies virtues: the **hair!**

Hair loss often has to do with the heart energy—so activating your heart energy as shown in this book will not only prevent hair loss (especially in men) but also let your mane shine.

Activate your heart energy and LIVE out of and from your HEART.

# Activating the Leo Energy Flow Heart Function Energy

**Left side:** (to treat another person sit on her right side)

Place the fingers of your left hand on your left energy lock number 11 and the fingers of your right hand on your left energy lock number 17. Keep this position for at least five minutes or until you feel the energy pulsing under your fingers and beginning to flow in your body.

**Right side:** Simply reverse the sequence (to treat another person sit on her left side)

Place the fingers of your right hand on your right energy lock number 11 and the fingers of your left hand on your right energy lock number 17. Keep this position for at least five minutes or until you feel the energy pulsing under your fingers and beginning to flow in your body.

Left Activation Heart Energy

# Flowpath of Heart Energy

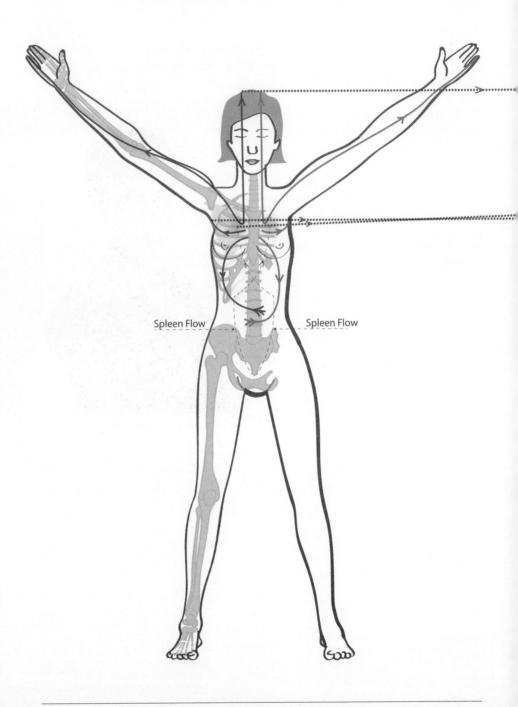

Spleen Flow                    Spleen Flow

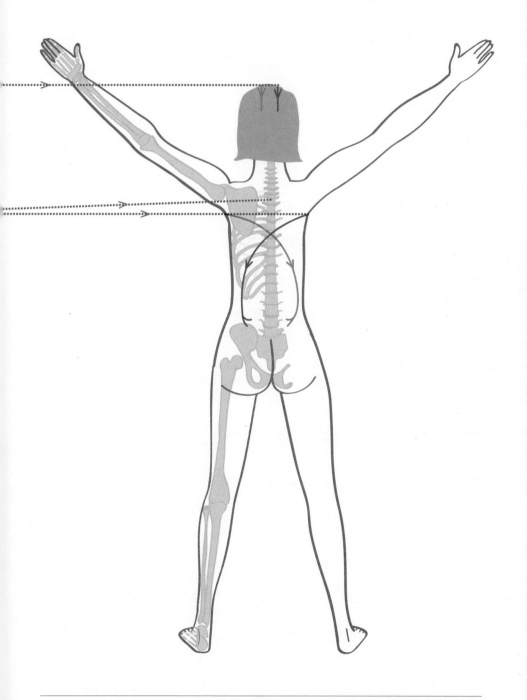

# The Opposition of Heart Function Energy and How They Cooperate

The opposition of Leo is Aquarius with its key energy gallbladder energy. It is the energies of fire (Leo) and air (Aquarius) that are working together here, with the air igniting the fire.

We already spoke about the cooperation of gallbladder and heart function energy in the 3rd Depth chapter under the heading "The Opposition of Gallbladder Energy and How They Cooperate," page 91. To give your heart energy an extra boost simply add the activation of gallbladder energy, thus enabling the fire of your heart to be kept alive and ignited.

# General Tips and Facts for Heart Days

**Massaging the Soul Gate:**

Your Leo Soul Gate is located on the **top of your head**—right on the crown chakra. Massage it gently in the morning (ideally after taking a shower) whenever the moon resides in Leo.

To do this, simply dip your fingers into some extra virgin oil (for example, almond or olive oil) and then massage the top of your head by gently moving the fingers clockwise.
While doing this, imagine your **Leo Soul Gate** in a yellow-golden-orange light, the color of Leo.

**Music/musical key:**

**A-sharp Major** is the musical key of Leo—one full tone up from its predecessor Cancer, which sounds in G-sharp Major.

It is difficult finding compositions in this musical key, but you may use B-flat Major instead, which is a more common musical key than the heart tone (musical key).

**Physical exercise:**

As mentioned already, you should avoid straining your body on Leo days—for the sake of your heart. However, it is still advisable to move—but simply prefer physical activation that is not too strenuous. Keep your head covered if you go outside since the sun's rays are much harsher and can burn you more easily on Leo days. (The same applies to Sagittarius days, which is also a double fire element, just like Leo. Leo is fire as is the element of 5th Depth!)

**Last but not least:**

Use Leo days to show yourself to the world. Get out there—shine and BE the success you were born to BE. Try to put important dates on Leo days. Dates like when you have to first introduce yourself for a new job, for example—where appearance matters and is essential.

Choosing the right date DOES make a difference. And even more so of course if you are properly tuned in.

I remember when I once went to a famous antiques market in London with my daughter. It was a Leo Saturday. I began the day by tuning my body into the Leo energy, activating my heart energy and dressed in red—the color of 5th Depth. While activating my heart energy, I visualized it in beautiful red light—spreading into my whole body and energizing it. On the antiques market a little later a vendor offered me a gift of valuable Chinese porcelain figures—as a gift. His response to my question how I came to this honor was simply—you have such a beautiful glow in your eyes. I smiled to myself thinking how the heart energy flows right through the eyes and how the eyes are known to be the "gate to spirit." Eyes don't lie, so if you want to know whether someone is lying, look him/her into the eyes—and thus straight into the heart—you will know if you have been told the truth or not.

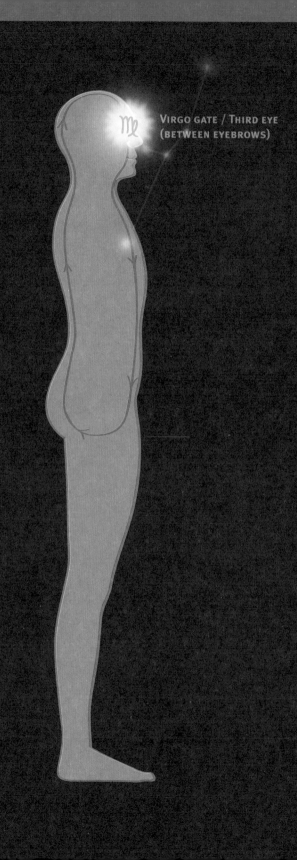

VIRGO GATE / THIRD EYE
(BETWEEN EYEBROWS)

# THE MOON OPENS THE COSMIC GATE OF
# VIRGO

*You Open Your Virgo Soul Gate through the
Vibration of Small Intestine Function Energy*

### Virgo says:
### "I analyze and distinguish"

Leo's heart flow transported the energy out of the heart into the hands, where the fire transforms into Earth and becomes "available to be rooted."

The **small intestine energy** is your key flow to open your Virgo Soul Gate at the third eye.

An open third eye enables you to **distinguish**—to distinguish between the TRUTH (your spiritual, eternal level) and the reality, the "effect" of the truth.

The ancient wise men knew that with an open third eye during the moment of death, the person passing on to the next level would remember his/her last life in every detail  and carry the knowledge not only into the afterlife, but also into the next life.

However, you do not have to wait until the moment of your passing on.

Activating your Virgo flow small intestine energy will enable you to "see through" the veil already now—to see from outside of the box, in the truest sense of the word.

To rise above our "small world thinking" is not exactly what you would think could be one of Virgo's or small intestine's attributes. Virgo is known to be able to be meticulous, especially about the "small" things others often don't notice or cannot be bothered to see.

However, it is Virgo's attribute to "open your spiritual sight"—supported by the Piscean liver energy—the opposition of Virgo.

Virgo's musical key is C Major—a beautiful and widely loved musical key praised by the Russian composer D. Schostakowitsch as the musical key bringing "peace and harmony" to man. Schostakowitsch (himself born under the sign of Virgo) used C Major as the musical key for one of his most famous compositions: the "Symphony of Leningrad"—a masterpiece meant to convey to the Russian the nearing of PEACE during the occupation of Leningrad at the end of the second world war.

**Peace** and **purity** are closely connected—and depend on each other—and Virgo's small intestine flow also restores purity, especially after both emotional as well as physical abuse.

*Virgo's small intestine flow restores purity after emotional and physical (sexual) abuse.*

Energetically, an abused person carries "a dark coat"—it is as if a dark layer covers the core of the person's being and prevents him from expressing the self.
Yes, it can be seen as a kind of protection after abuse; however, this protection also prevents the energy of Source to enter your life . . . and will after time leave you exhausted.

Activating Virgo's small intestine energy as shown in this book enables you to take the dark layer off and replace it by pure white light—white light that lets your SELF shine and express itself in reality in all its beauty!

Purity is also essential for a healthy and strong **immune system**. Doing the activation sequence of Virgo's small intestine energy as shown on page 171 is an excellent way to prevent a beginning cold from establishing itself within your system. It is the energy locks 11 (letting go of old garbage) and 13 (love thy enemy) that you open to activate the small intestine flow—two of the most powerful energy locks, opening and cleansing your whole being. Opening your shoulders (your angle of expression) and your heart chakra, since energy lock 13 (which on another level is associated with Scorpio's kidney energy the harmonizer of FEAR) is the heart chakra energy lock—the most important chakra for HEALING.

# Activating the Virgo Energy Flow
## Small Intestine Function Energy

**Left side:** (to treat another person sit on her right side)

Place the fingers of your left hand on your left energy lock number 11 and the fingers of your right hand on your right energy lock number 13. Keep this position for at least five minutes or until you feel the energy pulsing under your fingers and beginning to flow in your body.

**Right side:** Simply reverse the sequence (to treat another person sit on her left side)

Place the fingers of your right hand on your right energy lock number 11 and the fingers of your left hand on your left energy lock number 13. Keep this position for at least five minutes or until you feel the energy pulsing under your fingers and beginning to flow in your body.

Left Activation Small Intestine Energy

# Flowpath of Small Intestine Energy

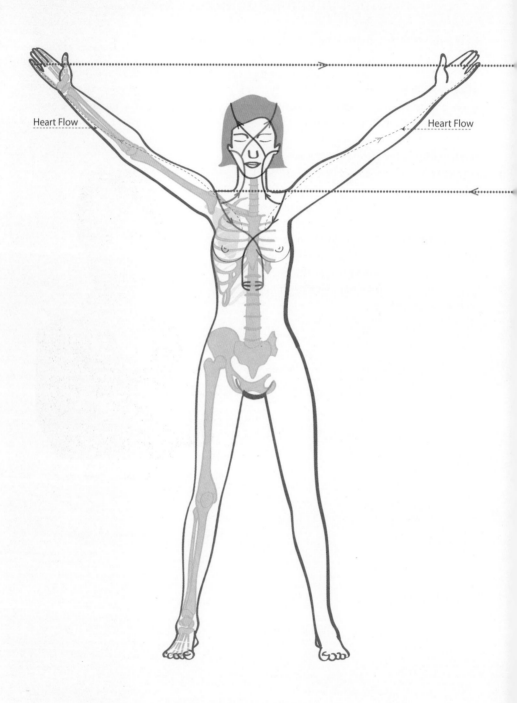

Heart Flow

Heart Flow

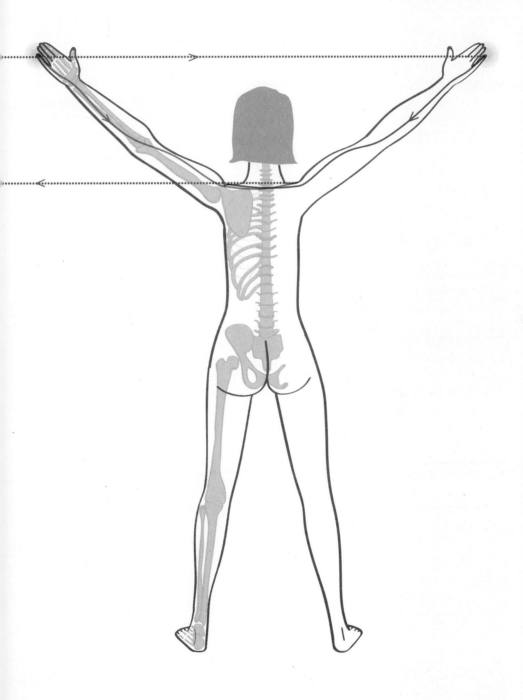

# The Opposition of Small Intestine
## Function Energy and How They Cooperate

The opposition of Virgo is Pisces with its key energy liver function flow. Both the liver function energy as well as the small intestine energy energize and boost your sight—both your physical as well as your spiritual eye sight. We spoke about this cooperation in our 3rd Depth chapter under the heading "The Opposition of Liver Energy and How They Cooperate," page 101. Give your small intestines energy that extra boost by also activating at least one side of your liver energy and open your vision to what truly IS!

# General Tips and Facts for
# **VIRGO DAYS**

**Massaging the Soul Gate:**

Your Virgo Soul Gate is located on the **third eye** between your eyebrows. Massage it gently in the morning (ideally after taking a shower) whenever the moon resides in Virgo.

To do this, simply dip your fingers into some extra virgin oil (for example, almond or olive oil) and then massage the area between your eyebrows clockwise.

While doing this, imagine your **Virgo Soul Gate** in indigo blue or crystal white. Crystal white is the color associated with the third eye from the original Indian chakra teachings. White is the color of purity and discernment—Virgo's most important virtues.

**Music/musical key:**

**C Major** is Virgo's musical key, and contrary to Virgo's predecessors, C Major is a much-used musical key by many famous and not-so-famous composers. Activate your Virgo flow while listening to a musical piece in C Major. Let the music embrace you as you embrace it and *become* the C major vibration.

**Physical exercise:**

Virgo days are 5th Depth days, so do not strain your body. Keep it "soft" and easy with Yoga or Tai Chi, both excellent ways to ground 5th Depth fire and take advantage of Virgo's Earth energy.

**Last but not least:**

Virgo days encourage and stimulate you to really go into detail, to be meticulous about your work.

Use the knowledge of this important gift of Virgo to do work that needs proper looking into. Since Virgo is also associated with purity and healthy living, Virgo days are a perfect time to generally switch to a more healthy lifestyle and diet. The other days of the month, however, should not be used as an excuse for you to "wait until the moon resides in Virgo" to live healthily. However, setting the goal and consciously beginning a proper change in your eating habits is aided by Virgo's energy, so Virgo days will help you to stick with your plans also in the future.

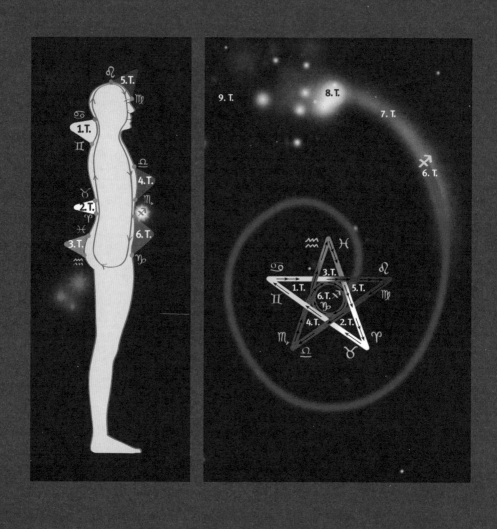

# 4th Depth—Blue Point-of-Star
## WATER

The MOON travels through the 4th Depth
and opens the cosmic gate of LIBRA followed
by the cosmic gate of SCORPIO.

For you this means that you reach SOURCE by opening your . . .

LIBRA Soul Gate *through* the vibration
of BLADDER Function Energy,

followed by your . . .

SCORPIO Soul Gate *through* the vibration
of KIDNEY Function Energy!

# The BLUE Point-of-Star and Its Element WATER!
## Deep Cleansing, Transformation, and Regeneration!

After igniting and rooting the spiritual fire, it is all about the cooling waters of 4th Depth, the water of LIFE, taking us back into the center of the five-pointed star—back to Source. If you have a look at the five-pointed star on illustration number 3 you can see that the blue point-of-star, our fifth and last point-of-star to unfold leads straight back into the center of the star, into the 6th Depth, the eternal beginning and rebirth of creation.

As such, 4th Depth is known—as is 3rd Depth, the initiator of the unfolding of the star—as a "bridge Depth," a Depth bridging the Earthly and the spiritual level of being.

4th Depth is all about **regeneration** and **deep transformation**. You may notice that you are more tired during the "blue" 4th Depth days. This is your body naturally reacting to the regenerating waters of 4th Depth. Listen to the wisdom of your body, and take it easy on the blue days. Go to bed early, get enough rest, especially during the 4th Depth hours between 4:00 p.m. and 8:00 p.m. (See also table II on page 37 for the star signs and their corresponding Depths, organs, musical keys, times, and ages.)

While resting, make sure to hold your index finger, your energizing finger for the 4th Depth.

Blue is the color of 4th Depth, and is it not interesting that "feeling blue" describes exactly the feeling of a disharmonized 4th Depth? Melancholy and depression are sure signs of your Soul asking for attention within 4th Depth, asking for the activation of bladder and kidney energy.

All Depths are essential—they are YOU.

However, since 4th Depth has as its primary task the cleansing of your whole body, which is essential to the proper functioning of all body functions, 4th Depth is seen among the most important Depths in the prevention and curing of any dis-ease.

It is like caring for your home—which, if you think about it, is the case—the home of your Soul.

Just as you probably like to keep your home nice and clean to accommodate its inhabitants, so should you strive to keep your body nice and clean—and the best way to do this besides a healthy diet and drinking plenty of good quality pure spring water or herbal teas, is the activation of your bladder and kidney function energies.

4th Depth—and especially the kidney energy—is also known as the Depth of destiny, with destiny being the tasks that your own Soul sends you.

Destiny in German is "Schicksal," a word that is put together from the verb "schicken" = to send/sending, and the ancient Germanic term for Soul, Sal—the Soul that sends its own tasks to "get back on track."

Getting back on track—or FINALLY on the path chosen by YOU yourself, chosen by your Soul—Destiny (or especially the German term "Schicksal") is often regarded as something to be afraid of, as something that "interrupts" the routine, and that strangely enough, is what many people fear most: the interruption of "routine," which on the other hand often brings misery.

Paradoxically, most people desire "change"—the hope to transform their lives into something better, but at the same time they fear nothing more than the act of change.

They, so to speak, want the result without the change, and that is not possible. The act of change . . . this is 4th Depth, the *ACT* of change, which at the same time is the goal already, just as the bible says.

To BE the FLOW is always the correct path; it is the path of your SOUL.

4th Depth is also the Depth of your **ancestors** and that which they have passed on and which you will pass on.

And, yes! It IS of course possible to transform that which has been "passed-on" to you. Anything can be transformed, and this is precisely what the waters of 4th Depth can and should be used for.

Imagine yourself under a waterfall of the cleanest, purest, and most beautiful water—the water of life, deeply cleansing and regenerating your whole being.

This is the power of 4th Depth, of its organs bladder function energy with its Soul Gate on the heart chakra, the main chakra for healing, and Scorpio's kidney energy with its Soul Gate the Solar plexus.

Two immensely powerful organ tools and Chakras—there to be used by YOU, to take LIFE into your own hands, and transform it to dance the chosen dance of your Soul on the chosen path of your Soul!

# Harmonizing the 4th Depth
## Index Finger

The "quickie method" of harmonizing 4th Depth is the index finger. Whenever the moon passes the blue area on the zodiac, your index finger is the finger that will harmonize your 4th Depth with its associated organs kidney energy and bladder energy and deeply cleanse your whole.

On another level, holding your index finger will open—amongst others—your energy lock 11, the main energy lock to clear and "release" your shoulders, which are one of the main body part for "storing stress"; relaxing your shoulders will enable the organ flows starting in the chest (the heart flow, the diaphragm flow, and the lung flow, as well as the finger flows[16] umbilicus function, large intestine function energy, and small intestine flow, to freely pass through the shoulders).

Wrap the fingers of your left hand around the index finger of your right hand and keep this position for a few minutes—ideally for twenty minutes, but even holding it for only three minutes already has a positive effect on your body functions and emotion.

Then change hands and wrap the fingers of your right hand around your left index finger. Again, keep this position for at least three to five minutes, again, ideally for twenty minutes!

Imagine your 4th Depth organs bladder and kidneys in vibrant blue light—and LOVE them! They will love you back and cleanse your whole being.

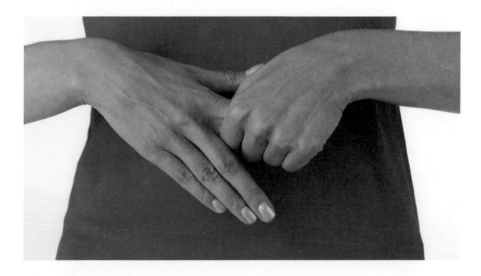

# General Tips for the Moon's Journey through the 4th Depth

- **Standing** up for a long time weakens your 4th Depth, as does too much talking in the morning. You talk with your tongue, and one branch of kidney energy (see on the graphic kidney flowpath the little side branches on the left and right side of the flow on the neck) flows right into your tongue. Talking generally weakens the kidney energy, which is why the real traditional Ayurveda cures suggest that the patient should refrain from talking for the duration of the cure—ideally for three weeks! Try it out for at least a whole morning—or—if you can manage a whole day and night, don't talk. Instead activate your kidney energy by holding your index finger or by simply sitting on your hands, thereby touching energy lock 25 on your seat bones. This simple "exercise" activates your 4th Depth organs bladder and kidney energy and totally regenerates you. It is also known as "jogging for the lazy," since it has the same effect as a physical workout without the effort. I describe and show this simple exercise in my wellness booklet *Wellness above the Clouds,* which is also available in Kindle format.

- **Blue** is the color of 4th Depth, and it is also known as the color of PEACE. Transforming fear brings an amazing feeling of PEACE, so BE the beautiful blue 4th Depth. Love your bladder, love your kidneys, and become a PEACEbringer!

- **Food/taste: Salt** stimulates your 4th Depth and especially the kidney energy. However, it needs to be unprocessed sea salt. And—as with everything—the principle of "the right dose" applies, meaning that too much will have the contrary effect. Try adding a little unprocessed sea salt to your food, or even start your day with a cleansing sea-salt-vitamin C drink. Simply add a little unprocessed sea salt to a glass of spring water with lemon juice to give the vitamin C boost. This drink is highly cleansing and will stimulate your digestion in the morning.

# Fourth Depth and Emotional Growth

**Fear** is the negative emotion of 4th Depth. It is the root of all negative emotions. A world without fear would be a world in harmony and peace. All wars start with unsolved fear. So, let's transform this fear, each and every one into

## LOVE, WISDOM, and GENTLENESS!

Ω LIBRA GATE / CENTER OF CHEST
(HEART CHAKRA)

# THE MOON OPENS THE COSMIC GATE OF
# LIBRA

*You Open Your Libra Soul Gate through the*
*Vibration of Bladder Function Energy*

### Libra says:
### "I balance."

When the moon travels on from Virgo's Soul Gate at the third eye, we reach the heart chakra, the center of healing, and harmony in man.

The heart chakra is the chakra of deep emotions. It is from here that we experience deepest emotions, such as LOVE and FEAR.

It is also here that we tend to close ourselves to "feelings" in general—after trauma and hurt.

The heart chakra is Libra's Soul Gate, which we open by activating the **bladder function energy.**

Bladder function energy is one of the most harmonizing and balancing organ flows there is. It is a very special flow in that it is the only organ flow covering the whole back of man.

Starting from the forehead, where it takes over from its predecessor small intestine energy, the bladder flow takes the energy over the top of the head, hereby relieving tensions in the head, into the ears (one of the main anti-ear-problem-flows), down the neck and the whole backside of the body.
Since the back is associated with the past, the bladder flow **clears your past** and enables you to finally make that step forward—that step in life that you may have wanted to do for quite a while but which so far you have not dared out of **fear**, with fear being the negative emotion of 4th Depth.

When a small child falls and hurts itself, it is a common practice to immediately put it on the potty to release the tension. The bladder flow releases tension and gives you a feeling of great **peace**.

For the activation sequence, you touch energy lock 12 with one hand and the coccyx with the other. 12 is the complete surrender to the higher will—*Thy will not mine*—with "mine" meaning the ego versus the true Self.

The bladder flow enables you to let go of deeply rooted fears and belief systems. It acts like a sparkling and cleansing water fall, **calming**, **soothing,** and at the same time **highly energizing.**

Bladder flow is one of the main flows for the strengthening, protection, and regeneration of the **nerves** and the **spine**. And of course for any back problems in general.

Back pain is the cry of the Soul to clear your past and to release fears. As such, the bladder flow can be seen as a "psychiatrist," helping you to come to terms with your own thoughts, balancing your thoughts and clearing them.

This is an attribute of all face flows, since all organ flows starting in the face belong to the element of Air—gallbladder flow (Aquarius), stomach flow (Gemini), and bladder flow (Libra)—and harmonize the thoughts.

Our own thoughts can at times be our own worst enemy.
Imagine your bladder in beautiful azure blue light while holding energy lock 12 at the neck and the coccyx at the same time. Love your bladder, and it will love you back and open your heart chakra at the same time.

A person with an open heart chakra is pure harmony and vibrant health.

# Activating the Libra Energy Flow
## Bladder Function Energy

**Left side:** (to treat another person sit on her left side)

Place the fingers of your right hand on your left energy lock number 12 and your left hand under your coccyx. Keep this position for at least five minutes or until you feel the energy pulsing under your fingers and beginning to flow in your body.

**Right side:** Simply reverse the sequence (to treat another person sit on her right side)

Place the fingers of your left hand on your right energy lock number 12 and your right hand under your coccyx. Keep this position for at least five minutes or until you feel the energy pulsing under your fingers and beginning to flow in your body.

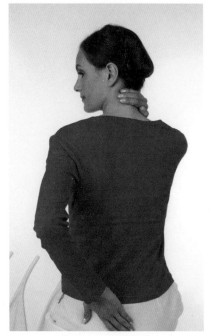

Left Activation
Bladder Energy

# Flowpath of Bladder Energy

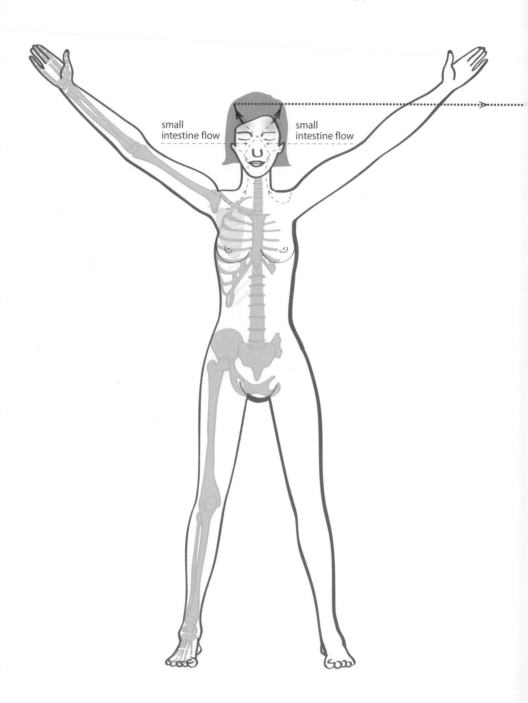

small intestine flow

small intestine flow

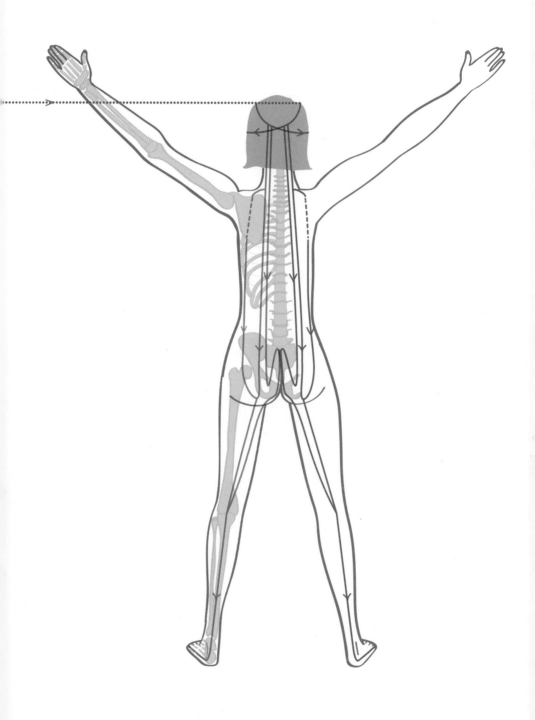

# The Opposition of Bladder Function Energy and How They Cooperate

The opposition of Libra is Aries with its key energy lung flow. In our Aries chapter we've already spoken about the cooperation of lung and bladder energy under the header "The Opposition of Lung Function Energy and How They Cooperate." Both organ energies have a strong connection to the chest and the heart chakra with the lung flow being more "physical" and the bladder flow and its Soul Gate heart chakra addressing the issue from a more spiritual view. Keeping your lung and bladder functions in harmony will greatly enhance your vitality, strengthen your nervous system, and give you an overall sense of feeling "at ease with yourself." So, give your body that extra boost on Libra days by adding at least one side of the lung function activation sequence; see page 114–115.

## General Tips and Facts for
## LIBRA DAYS

**Massaging the Soul Gate:**

Your Libra Soul Gate is located on the **heart chakra**. Massage it gently in the morning (ideally after taking a shower) whenever the moon resides in Libra.

To do this, simply dip your fingers into some extra virgin oil (for example, almond or olive oil) and then gently massage the center of your sternum.

While doing this, imagine your **Libra Soul Gate** in emerald green or a light pink, the colors of the Soul Gate of Libra and the heart chakra.

**Music/musical key:**

**D Major** is Libra's musical key—a beautiful and powerful musical key giving you self- esteem, energizing your nerves, and at the same time aiding your voice.

**Physical exercise:**

A relaxing and detoxing back massage may not be regarded as a "sport" but is the perfect treat to enjoy during the days when the moon resides in the cosmic gate of Libra. The bladder flow, as you know, flows down the back, so massaging the back following bladder's flowpath will greatly enhance its positive virtues and enable you to fully use the cosmic power for detoxification and regeneration.

**Last but not least:**

With Libra's amazing balancing and calming properties, Libra days are ideal for "calming the waters" with people you were having problems with or where things need to be harmonized. Activate your Libra energy, BE the flow and the open heart chakra, and approach the persons you want to make and have peace with. The whole universe will aid you and enable you to enjoy vibrant and harmonious relationships.

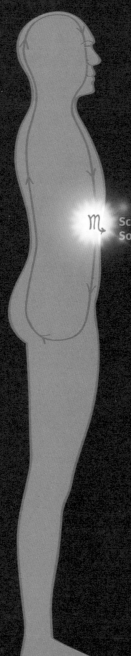

SCORPIO GATE /
SOLARPLEXUS

# THE MOON OPENS THE COSMIC GATE OF
# SCORPIO

*You Open Your Scorpio Soul Gate through the*
*Vibration of Kidney Function Energy*

### Scorpio says:
### "I transform and re-create myself."

Let it flow! BE the flow! Scorpio's **kidney energy** wants to **flow** and **transform!**

With Scorpio you are again crossing the bridge between the visible and the non-visible realms. You are about to re-enter the center of your five-pointed star—the core of your being.

And as is the case before "coming home," you should cleanse yourself properly and let go of anything no longer necessary for the onward journey.

Kidney energy does just that. It is the powerful "washing machine" of your body, cleansing and at the same time highly energizing and regenerating.

Imagine yourself as a plant deeply rooted within the ground. Kidney energy is these roots . . . it is your roots transporting the "juice of life" from the feet . . . from Earth . . . up the whole front body, through the sexual organs, energizing them (yes, kidney energy is one of the most important organ flows for anything to do with reproduction), flowing on through the **eyes**, energizing your eyes, continuing over the head, and down the back of your head and neck (energy lock number 4 at the first cervical vertebrae has a strong connection to the water element), and down the back, about one centimeter next to your spine on both sides, obviously (as you know by now, we always have a right and a left organ flow).

As such, kidney energy is the only organ flow flowing both up and down—although it still is considered an ascending flow since the ascending part is the main part of the kidney flow.

The Latin word *stamina* (Latin, plural of "stāmen thread," i.e., the life-threads spun by the Fates) is the perfect description of the kidney flow's characteristics: Stamina means *strength, enduring, and resilient.*

Exactly what you need for success in any part of life. A person may have the greatest ideas (specifically linked to the Pisces, Aquarius, and Gemini energy) but if he/she cannot manifest (cancer/spleen) these ideas and carry them right through to completion (kidney energy) even the greatest genius will not enjoy the success of seeing his/her initial spark manifest on Earth.

The Solar plexus, Scorpio's Soul Gate, is known as the center of POWER.

Power; what, however, is this?

Is it the ability to "reign over other people and use their resources" . . . or the ability to BE SOURCE yourself and have an unlimited pool of energy available for you to use?

It is of course the latter one.

Using other people is a sign of weakness and fear—the negative aspect and emotion of 4th Depth.

A clean and open Solar plexus will enable you to be powerful without ever exploiting or using other people. Kidney energy in harmony gives you a sense of natural authority that will automatically inspire others—inspire AND empower them, since true power is the gate to the infinite pool of energy to SOURCE itself. True power IS the Source, and that is the true life goal of each and every one of us.

# Activating the Scorpio Energy Flow
## Kidney Function Energy

**Left side:** (to treat another person sit on her right side)

Wrap the fingers of your right hand around your left little toe and place your left hand under your coccyx. Keep this position for at least five minutes or until you feel the energy pulsing under your fingers and beginning to flow in your body.

**Right side:** Simply reverse the sequence (to treat another person sit on her left side)

Wrap the fingers of your left hand around the right little toe and place your right hand under your coccyx. Keep this position for at least five minutes or until you feel the energy pulsing under your fingers and beginning to flow in your body.

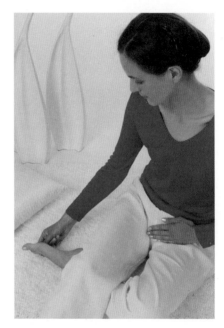

Left Activation Kidney Energy

# Flowpath of Kidney Energy

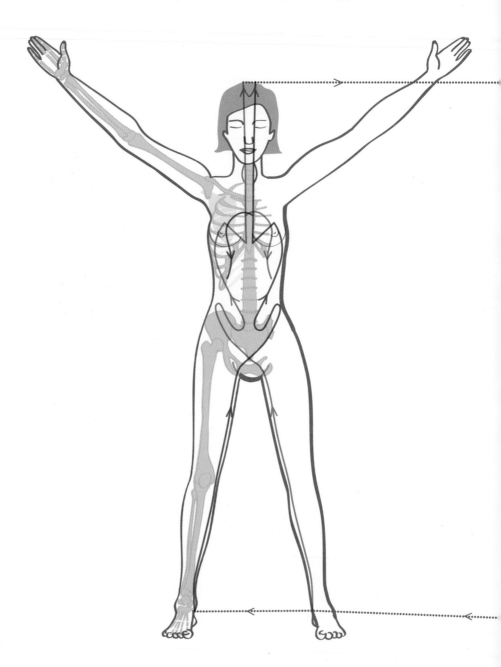

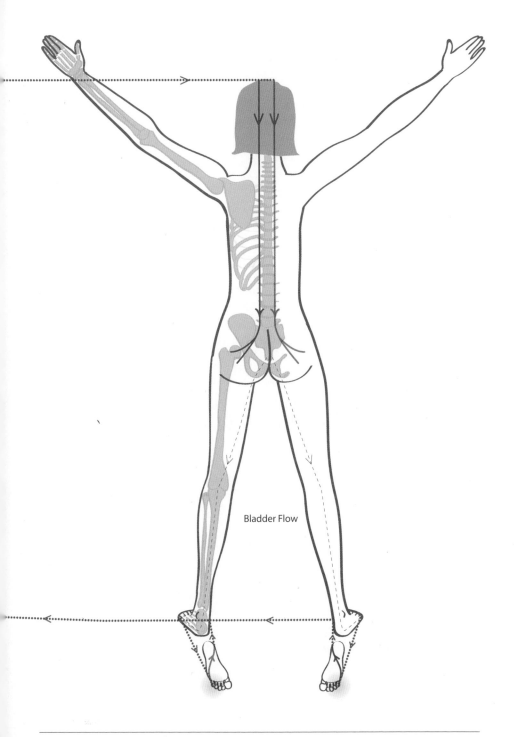

Bladder Flow

# The Opposition of Kidney Function Energy and How They Cooperate

Scorpio's opposition is Taurus—with its key energy large intestine energy. Both organ functions—kidney and large intestine—are essential for the detoxification process of the body.

A sluggish large intestine energy will have an impact both on your wellbeing (you will feel tired and generally unwell) as well as on your appearance, since skin problems are in most cases linked to large intestine and its ability to keep your system clean.

Kidney energy cleanses the large intestine, and the large intestine aids kidney energy through the position of its Soul Gate, which is located exactly on the same level on the back of your body as Scorpio's Soul Gate in the front.

By keeping large intestine and kidney energy flowing smoothly, you keep the center of your being open and able to GIVE and RECEIVE . . . your Solar plexus, the power center of your body.

So, give yourself that extra boost by adding at least one side of large intestine energy activation, see page 126, while the moon resides in Scorpio.

## General Tips and Facts for
## SCORPIO DAYS

**Massaging the Soul Gate:**

Your Scorpio Soul Gate is the Solar plexus. Massage it gently in the morning (ideally after taking a shower) whenever the moon resides in Scorpio.

To do this, simply dip your fingers into some extra virgin oil (for example, almond or olive oil) and then gently massage the area beneath the sternum.

While doing this, imagine your **Scorpio Soul Gate** in the color of its chakra—yellow, or, if you wish, in red, since according to the traditional Indian chakra colors, red is the true color of Solar plexus—which by the way also corresponds to the color of Scorpio, often seen as red, something that you will even notice in the sky on Scorpio days, since on Scorpio evenings the color generally boasts a stunning red!

**Music/musical key:**

**E Major** is Scorpio's musical key—and from here we will not go up a full tone, but only a half tone, to F Major, Sagittarius's musical key. It is the "point of return," so to speak, since from the next step on, the moon will change its direction again from descending to ascending. Isn't it amazing? The moon's direction of travel can be *heard* through the musical keys of the gates he is passing through. It shows us exactly that in Sagittarius a cycle ends AND begins anew and that the ascending direction will change into descending in the opposition of Sagittarius–Gemini, since between Taurus (E-flat Major) and Gemini (F-sharp Major) we have a tone and a half instead of the usual half tone between the changes.

Listen to or play a musical piece in E Major while the moon resides in Scorpio—and BE the vibration given to you by the Cosmos!

**Physical exercise:**

Scorpio days are days of deep relaxation—and should be used as such. Asian disciplines like, for example, Tai-Chi or Aikido, are ideal on these days—as they are simply relaxing, **also** holding your index finger and not talking for half a day, a whole day, or even two or three days if you can manage. Your body will thank you for it with deep regeneration.

**Last but not least:**

BE THE FLOW! is Scorpio's motto! Let go of anything that hinders you on your onward path!

On Scorpio days you may notice that unplanned things happen, or that new people enter your life, and others go, and that you may feel that you want to "close a chapter in your life."

Let Scorpio's mighty kidney energy take its course—or rather, let it get YOU back on track, onto the path chosen by your own Soul. By YOU!

BE the FLOW OF LIFE, constantly cleansing, regenerating, transforming, creating, and recreating itself and the wonders you hope will unfold!

# CONGRATULATIONS!

You have completed your first transformational cycle with the moon—a cycle given to you by the moon, which not only determines your life, but which actually *corresponds to* and *enables* physical existence.

By consciously tuning into this cycle on a regular basis—yes, *regular* is important, since creation is an ongoing, eternal process—you merge with the cosmic[1] order and become a conscious creator yourself.

Being a conscious creator means that you yourSELF consciously create your reality from Source—using the 12 tools of your Soul.

This does not mean that you may automatically become a millionaire simply because you wish to be a millionaire. It means that you fulfil that which your Soul has chosen to fulfil, so in other words, it means doing and fulfilling that which your TRUE self desires as opposed to what your "Ego" wants.

If becoming a millionaire is what yourSELF has chosen, then the tuning into the cosmic symphony of creation will enable you to reach this goal quicker and easier than without "being in the flow."

*Being in tune* enables you to clearly *see* and respond to your chosen path and to also *understand* WHY certain things are happening in your life—WHY you keep meeting the same kind of people or experiencing the same hurts over and over again.

And *understanding* this, the message behind these events and persons, which in reality are simply "mirrors" of your own energy, trying to tell you something, enables you to *transform* your life—to live it more "directly" without having to make painful "deviations" to reach your goal.

The way you live and experience your life is determined by the way your organs (tools of your Soul) function.

The moment you consciously *grasp* your organs—tools of your Soul—a miraculous transformation takes place. A transformation to GRATITUDE, understanding, higher energy levels, increased wellbeing, health, and a younger and fresher appearance.

Your life, your relationships, and of course your whole body are a direct result of how you use the tools of your Soul.

Your organs—or more precise, the way you USE your organs—determines your LIFE, and this fact is the key to yourSELF.

# Be the Cosmic Code of Creation!

What does it mean to *be* the Cosmic Code of Creation?

It means precisely what you have been shown in this book—to *tune* into the moon as the cosmic leader of cosmic life . . . of nature and humanity . . .

. . . and to unfold yourself through the Depths of your being through the 12 gates of your Soul.

The 12 Soul Gates are the principle of cosmos and the principle of physical existence.

Symbolically their description can be found in most ancient books of wisdom. The bible speaks of the 12 Apostles, many legends speak of 12 tasks, the 12 tasks to be fulfilled to reach enlightenment . . .

12 is THE cosmic number of creation. It is the higher vibration of 3, since 1 plus 2 is 3 . . . another spark and another opportunity to fulfil your potential.

Activating the cosmic code of creation is a holy procedure, just as the whole of nature, creation, every living cell is holy.

If you begin to treat your body as precisely this: the holy product of a holy eternal Source which is YOU, then not only your body but indeed your whole life will begin a miraculous transformation.

There will be a shift from "being the product of an unknown source" to "creating the product YOU desire out of the SOURCE that YOU yourSELF are and are CONSCIOUS of!"

Giving your organs = instruments of your Soul, the daily love and attention they deserve will enable you to become the magician using his/her 12 tools and the 4 elements of the Zodiac.

Anybody who is familiar with the Tarot knows the Major Arcana I, the Magician. The Magician is someone who *knows* and *uses* the four elements laid out before him/her on a table (his/her life). (*Rider Waite*).

The 4 is the key number of creation. It is manifestation itself. And by using these four elements of life, the Magician (You!) lets his/her life blossom and fulfils his/her potential.

By following the moon and tuning into its vibration, you unfold your star, your potential.

And this is done in exactly the cosmic order as in nature, since most five-petalled flowers unfold in exactly the sequence as you unfold your star. Take a look at the five-pointed star on page 35. The points are numbered A, B, C, D, E.

The sequence of the moon, the sequence in which we unfold the star, however, is not A, B, C, D, E . . . but A, C, E, B, D.

It is the cosmic order of creation, which—if you look deeper—creates **4** golden triangles (**3**) (see the chart on page 35) with 4 being the number needed to let the 3, the spark, evolve to become the **12.**

**12** being the higher 3 (1+2=3), the 3 that has attained—or rather—re-gained, wisdom and the ability to look from *above,* from Source— . . . the SOURCE that YOU yourSELF are, and have always been, and will always BE!

I AM
LOVE, LIGHT, and VIBRANT HEALTH!
With love,

Irene

# Symbols and Abbreviations

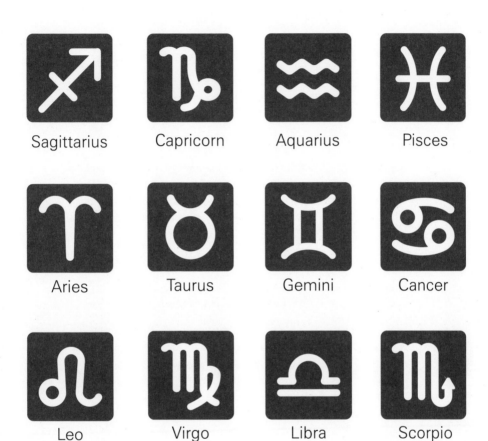

| | | | |
|---|---|---|---|
| Sagittarius | Capricorn | Aquarius | Pisces |
| Aries | Taurus | Gemini | Cancer |
| Leo | Virgo | Libra | Scorpio |

Abbreviation: T. = Depth
(From the German word "Tiefe" for "Depth")

# Endnotes

1. Diagram number 3 shows the five-pointed star of Man with each of the star points being a Depth, unfolding itself out of 6th Depth (center of the Star), the womb of creation. For the Pythagoreans the five-pointed Star was the holy symbol of Health. The five-pointed star holds the secret and the key to creation.

2. In Chinese philosophy the 5 elements are known as Wu Xing.

3. Diagram number 6 shows the Large Energy Cycle with the 4 element groups. You find it in the graphics part of this book, page 38.

4. Opposing star signs: Your opposition or opposing sign (gate) is the one six months away from your sign, for example Aries is the opposition to Libra because it is the sign of April, six months ahead of October, the month of Libra—it is the sign located "opposite" on the zodiac.

5. See also diagram "Flowpath of the Diaphragm Function Energy," page 57.

6. For recapitulation: The anatomical position used in many Far East Asian healing arts is an upright standing person with the arms pointed towards the sky and with hands pointing to the front. This is the reason why an energy flow flowing from the chest area to the tips of the fingers is also called an ascending energy flow.

7. Orange is the color for the umbilicus function energy since the color of the tone G (the key tone of the umbilicus function's musical key) would be orange; see also chapter umbilicus function energy.

8. The longer you hold the position, the better! If you know you have a problem with an organ, it is advisable to hold the position for 15–20 minutes, which will give it that "extra boost"!

9. The energy flowing from the fingers to the face and (or) chest is considered "descending," since in Far East Asian philosophy and medicine man is shown with the arms pointed upwards.

10. The longer you hold the positions the better. However, even doing the exercises just 5 minutes will harmonize your energies.

11. The longer you hold the positions the better. However, even doing the exercises just 5 minutes will harmonize your energies.

12. The longer you hold the positions the better. However, even doing the exercises just 5 minutes will harmonize your energies.

13. The longer you hold the positions the better. However, even doing the exercises just 5 minutes will harmonize your energies.

14. The longer you hold the positions the better. However, even doing the exercises just 5 minutes will harmonize your energies.

15. The longer you hold the positions the better. However, even doing the exercises just 5 minutes will harmonize your energies.

16. Finger flows are the organ flows starting in the Hands. See also the diagram on page 40.

17. The ancient greek word cosmos means order.

**IRENE LAURETTI** is a German Italian energy-healing therapist. In her work she combines the moon, Tarot, and numerology with the ancient healing arts of the Far East to create a unique way to discover the Self and heal from within. Using these self-healing arts herself, Irene found the moon to be the missing link to total health and well-being. After a near-death experience, the wisdom of the moon and the cosmic code of creation were revealed to her. This, along with her healing experience, enabled her to understand why and how the moon affects us and why humans function the way they do. Irene's German-language books are all bestsellers and have already helped thousands of readers. For information and to book a counseling session, see Irene's webpage at www.irenelauretti.com or email her directly at irene.lauretti@yahoo.com